"I have systematically read the best Christmas books, but this is the one I have been waiting for. Rather than addressing just the cultural or theological aspects, Emily Hunter McGowin brilliantly connects them. For those who sometimes feel uncertain about how to navigate the holiday season, *Christmas: The Season of Life and Light* illuminates a faithful, Yuletide lane with the festive glow of twinkling lights."

Timothy Larsen, editor of *The Oxford Handbook of Christmas*

"I've wanted to make Christmas more spiritual without nagging about nonreligious symbols or being an impolite guest while partygoers sip champagne to the melody of 'Chestnuts Roasting on an Open Fire.' Thank you, Emily, for showing the way! *Christmas: The Season of Life and Light* both reveals the history and mystery of the birth of Jesus and shows us how to celebrate it in truly spiritual ways."

Todd Hunter, founding bishop of the diocese of Churches for the Sake of Others and author of *What Jesus Intended: Finding True Faith in the Rubble of Bad Religion*

"As a pastor I used to dread the Christmas season, in fear that the church had lost the narrative. In *Christmas*, Emily Hunter McGowin masterfully blends her theological mind and her pastoral heart and goes a long way toward reclaiming the story and its meaning. She breaks the knot of syrupy sentimentalism and rampant commercialism, not with a snub nor judgment but with a generous resanctification of our traditions that creates space for us to experience the life and light of this treasured time of year. With this book in hand, I can't wait to enter into the next Christmas season!"

Jin Cho, Anglican priest and cohost of *The Micah Podcast*

"Emily Hunter McGowin's *Christmas* is a beautiful guide through a rich season in the church calendar. With grace and wisdom, McGowin unpacks history, metaphor, tradition, and contemporary illustrations of the holiday in a way that is both profoundly insightful and delightfully readable. This is a great companion for laypeople, Christian educators, pastors, and students alike, written with an invitational spirit of discovery. I'll be recommending *Christmas* far and wide!"

Courtney Ellis, pastor and author of *Happy Now*

"This book is a gift. As Christians, we have all experienced the challenge of navigating culture while living a liturgical life during the Christmas season. Emily McGowin's volume on Christmas for the Fullness of Time series offers a faithful way through by distilling some of the most important biblical and theological insights of what is revealed to us about God from Advent to Christmas. In this beautifully written book, McGowin offers a discerning and insightful guide for deepening Christian faith and practice during the season of Christmas."

Jennifer Powell McNutt, Franklin S. Dyrness Associate Professor in Biblical and Theological Studies at Wheaton College

"Theologically rich, historically anchored, liturgically alert, socially alert, wide ranging, culturally connected, and all this always with an eye on the church—such expressions reveal the value of this small, timely, and wonderful book about Christmas. Buy it during Advent, wrap it up under the tree, and give your friends or family a gift that will stimulate their faith during Christmastide. The gift of Christmas will be made more generous by the gift of this book."

Scot McKnight, professor of New Testament at Northern Seminary and author of *The Jesus Creed*

"Emily McGowin's *Christmas* has something to offer everyone: longtime Christians, people who are new to the faith, those who worship in liturgical spaces, Christians in nondenominational spaces, even non-Christians. It is a beautiful reminder of what Christmas is about at the core. McGowin's personal stories about faith and family plus her knowledge of theology and church history make a book that is enjoyable, educational, and full of hope. It's the perfect book to read on your own or with a group in preparation for the season of Christmas."

Kimberly Deckel, priest and executive pastor at Church of the Cross Austin

"Those of us who are tired or cynical at Christmastime need this book by Emily McGowin, who gives Christmas back to us without stinginess or sentimentality, inviting us to wonder at the Word made flesh. McGowin brings the wisdom of the theological adept, the pastoral heart of the priest, and the tenderness of the disciple to help us understand what it means to worship a newborn king."

Beth Felker Jones, professor of theology at Northern Seminary and author of *Practicing Christian Doctrine*

"The seasons of the Christian year have been a wonderful discipleship tool that the church has used to celebrate the major events of the life of Jesus and the kingdom of God for centuries. Christmas is my favorite season of the Christian year. I love the colors, sights, and smells of the season. Emily McGowin has written a wonderful book that reminds us of the beauty and the mystery of the virgin birth of our Savior Jesus Christ."

Winfield Bevins, author of *Liturgical Mission* and director of church planting at Asbury Theological Seminary

Emily Hunter McGowin

Esau McCaulley, SERIES EDITOR

Christmas

The Season of Life and Light

Fullness of Time series

An imprint of InterVarsity Press
Downers Grove, Illinois

InterVarsity Press
P.O. Box 1400 | Downers Grove, IL 60515-1426
ivpress.com | email@ivpress.com

InterVarsity Press® is the publishing division of InterVarsity Christian Fellowship/USA®. For more information, visit intervarsity.org.

All Scripture quotations, unless otherwise indicated, are taken from The Holy Bible, New International Version®, NIV®. Copyright © 1973, 1978, 1984, 2011 by Biblica, Inc.™ Used by permission of Zondervan. All rights reserved worldwide. www.zondervan.com. The "NIV" and "New International Version" are trademarks registered in the United States Patent and Trademark Office by Biblica, Inc.™

While any stories in this book are true, some names and identifying information may have been changed to protect the privacy of individuals.

Figure 1. Iconostasis of the nativity, by anonymous Russian iconographer, c. 1497 / Wikimedia Commons.

The publisher cannot verify the accuracy or functionality of website URLs used in this book beyond the date of publication.

Cover design: David Fassett
Interior design: Daniel van Loon

ISBN 978-1-5140-0040-3 (print) | ISBN 978-1-5140-0041-0 (digital)

Printed in the United States of America ∞

Library of Congress Cataloging-in-Publication Data
A catalog record for this book is available from the Library of Congress.

29 28 27 26 25 24 23 | 11 10 9 8 7 6 5 4 3 2 1

For Susan, my mother-in-love,

who loved Christmas more than anyone I know.

Contents

The Fullness of Time

SERIES PREFACE

ESAU McCAULLEY, SERIES EDITOR

Christians of all traditions are finding a renewed appreciation for the church year. This is evident in the increased number of churches that mark the seasons in their preaching and teaching. It's evident in the families and small groups looking for ways to recover ancient practices of the Christian faith. This is all very good. To assist in this renewal, we thought Christians might find it beneficial to have an accessible guide to the church year, one that's more than a devotional but less than an academic tome.

The Fullness of Time project aims to do just that. We have put together a series of short books on the seasons and key events of the church year, including Advent,

Christmas, Epiphany, Lent, Easter, and Pentecost. These books are reflections on the moods, themes, rituals, prayers, and Scriptures that mark each season.

These are not, strictly speaking, devotionals. They are theological and spiritual reflections that seek to provide spiritual formation by helping the reader live fully into the practices of each season. We want readers to understand how the church is forming them in the likeness of Christ through the church calendar.

These books are written from the perspective of those who have lived through the seasons many times, and we'll use personal stories and experiences to explain different aspects of the season that are meaningful to us. In what follows, do not look for comments from historians pointing out minutiae. Instead, look for fellow believers and evangelists using the tool of the church year to preach the gospel and point Christians toward discipleship and spiritual formation. We pray that these books will be useful to individuals, families, and churches seeking a deeper walk with Jesus.

An Introduction

At the Church of the Nativity in Bethlehem, you can go and see the small patch of earth where, according to tradition, the Virgin Mary gave birth to Jesus. The Greek Orthodox and Armenian Apostolic churches currently maintain the site. You have to descend countless stone stairways and traverse labyrinthine passageways, past rich brocades and hanging lamps, to reach the hallowed cave. I have not visited it myself, but I'm told the grotto smells of damp earth and burning oil while the air reverberates with the sounds of chanting and singing from the many chambers above. Beneath the main stone altar, a fourteen-point silver star surrounds a circular hole marking the spot where, according to the Latin inscription, "Jesus Christ was born to the Virgin Mary." To touch the mark, you are forced to kneel and crouch, leaning beneath a fringed satin drape to place a finger into the hole. Within the recess, according to tradition, lies the stone on which Mary lay as she pushed the infant Christ into the world.[1]

Outside the church is Manger Square, where Catholic Midnight Mass is celebrated on December 24 (and Orthodox Christmas Eve thirteen days later). Christmas Eve events in Manger Square are attended by thousands of people and broadcast live around the world. Every year locals and pilgrims gather to sing Christmas carols, surrounded by countless twinkling lights and multicolored decorative flags. Festivities officially begin when the Latin patriarch of Jerusalem enters the city near Rachel's Tomb and makes his way through the streets, accompanied by parades of children and youth. At the conclusion of Midnight Mass at the Church of Saint Catherine, he carries an icon of the child Jesus through the square to the Nativity Grotto in the depths of the church. The icon is placed over the silver star, marking the time and place of Christ's arrival in our world.

Most of us will never see the Grotto of the Nativity or celebrate Christmas in Manger Square. But it is good to recall that the place Christ was born is not simply a soft-focused backdrop to our favorite Christmas stories and hymns but a living, vibrant place with an ongoing

Christian community. Today Bethlehem is no longer a small village but has about twenty-five thousand inhabitants and occupies a central place in the religious life of Palestinian Christians.[2] Though it's been over two thousand years, the humble arrival of the Son of God continues to capture imaginations today. When we seek to draw near to the mystery of Christmas—as we are doing with this small book—we're joining a millions-strong procession of other Christians from all over the world who have been worshiping the newborn king for millennia.

I didn't have this global perspective when I was a child. An ocean away from Bethlehem and in a nonreligious home, I grew up knowing little about Christmas. But I still considered it my favorite holiday—and not just because of the presents. Somehow I knew there was something extraordinary happening from sundown Christmas Eve to sunup Christmas Day. I could feel in my bones the "deep magic" in the celebration of Christ's birth—as though my young body sensed in Christmas a point of rendezvous for God and humankind. Once the Holy Spirit found me and brought me into Christ's church, Christmas took on even more significance. Like Saint Augustine, I was drawn to faith in Christ through the marvelous beauty of the Word made flesh—that the Son "of the Father's love begotten" was born of a virgin in a backwater Middle Eastern town. It was the most magnificent story I had ever heard. It still is.

Yet for all my love of Christmas, it remains difficult to write about. For most of us, the season is hopelessly intertwined with sentimentality, nostalgia, and commercialism. Christmas overflows with vivid memories—some good and some not so good—and elevated expectations— some healthy and some not so healthy. Like Dr. Seuss's Grinch perched on Mount Crumpit, our respective imaginations have loaded the Christmas "sleigh" with a surplus of sights, smells, sounds, and tastes: soft candlelight, aromatic wassail, singing choirs, decadent pies and puddings, the crinkle of shiny wrapping paper, and much more. Even though Christmas belongs to the universal church that spans the globe, there's no denying that those of us living in the West experience the season in ways decidedly different from, for instance, the Palestinian Christians gathered in Bethlehem's Manger Square. We know instinctively that Christmas is more than shopping mall Santas, silver bells, and snow-flocked trees, but such things are so entangled with our impressions of Christmas that it's hard to know where those things end and Christmas—the real-deal, traditional, transcultural season of the church year—begins. What are we to do?

The first thing is to acknowledge that this is our reality and do our best, by God's grace, to make our peace with it. There's simply no way to fully disentangle Christmas from our embodied and encultured experiences of it. We must pursue an understanding and appreciation of Christmas in the midst of our memories, expectations, and hang-ups. After all, at the center of the mystery of Christmas is the astonishing fact that God has come to dwell with us. God has seen fit to grace our world with God's presence—not just once but for all time—in Jesus Christ. So God's loving embrace extends to our particulars—noses and toes, meals and gifts, decorations and gift-giving. Even if we could leave our embodied existence and all its memories behind, God would not have us do so. It is precisely the real stuff of daily life—even the heavily commercialized season of Christmas—that God means to redeem in Christ. As Madeleine L'Engle says in her poem "First Coming," "He did not wait for the perfect time. He came when the need was deep and great. . . . He came with Love: Rejoice! Rejoice!"[3]

Despite the sentimentality surrounding Christmas, its focus—and the focus of the whole liturgical calendar—is the triune God. To give ourselves to the observance of the church year is to give ourselves to an education, a formative submersion, in the Trinity. Each season reveals something more of God's truth, goodness, and beauty (though the fullness of God we will never fully comprehend). Christmas reveals to us the God of the great exchange, the God of the poor, the God of creation and re-creation, the God of life and light, the God of the crèche and the cross. "He came with Love," indeed, and we are compelled to worship and serve him in return. Christmastide offers us one more way to do so.

The beauty of the liturgical calendar is that it provides a substantial length of time to prepare to approach the mystery of Christmas. We call this time Advent. But preparation for Christmas was not the original focus of Advent. Early in the church's history, Advent was primarily concerned with the second coming of Christ—looking beyond history's horizon to the final judgment of all things. In its modern iteration, though, Advent tends to be observed as preparation for Christmas, even as it retains the emphasis on watching and waiting for Christ's return. Advent calls our attention to the prolonged anticipation of God's people both for the first and second comings of the Messiah. And by engaging in practices of repentance during Advent, our bodies and souls are prepared for the celebratory practices of worship and feasting during Christmas.

Many of us may find it easier to participate in Advent (and Lent, its springtime complement). Human life is marked by suffering, and celebration doesn't always come easily to a people acquainted with sorrow and hope deferred. Despite the gains of modernity, the dreadful beasts of conquest, war, famine, plague, and death continue to stalk the earth. And now with the help of mass media we are perhaps more aware than ever of the breadth and depth of the anguish they inflict. No amount of money or power can shield us from the vulnerability of being human. Sickness, heartbreak, and loss, it seems, are the price we pay for existence. Nevertheless, the church calendar ensures that, no matter how long and dark our Advent, the season of waiting always gives way to the season of wonder. By God's abounding grace, Christmas still arrives every year—somehow or other, it comes just the same.[4]

In the chapters that follow I offer an entryway into the liturgical season of Christmas. I do so by meditating on what the Scriptures, practices, and prayers of the season reveal about God. I draw on a variety of other resources in the Christian tradition, too, including rituals, music, poetry, and art. The Festival of the Incarnation is divine in origin—God became human in Jesus Christ—but decidedly human in practice. How Christians have celebrated the coming of Christ has inevitably evolved over the past two millennia and varies considerably from place to place. So along the way I also provide stories and historical background to help us better understand the rituals and symbols we now consider essential to the season.

Of course, a work of this sort is inherently limited by the perspective and context of its author. I write as an Anglican priest-theologian and professor in the midwestern United States. While I respect and appreciate the differences between Eastern and Western church approaches to the holiday, mine remains decidedly (though, I hope, humbly) Western. Though I write from the broader Anglican tradition and intentionally draw on its assets, I seek to retain an ecumenical spirit.

Much more could be said than what I've been able to include here. So along the way I'll offer recommendations for further reading for those who may wish to explore more on their own. My hope is that Christians of all traditions will find this little book illuminating and edifying as they seek to faithfully observe the holy days of Christmas.

May the glory of the Word made flesh abound in our lives and resound throughout the world!

The Origins of Christmas

Christmas (a shortened form of "Christ's mass") has been an embattled holiday for much of its history—and not just because talking heads on TV like to argue about the "war on Christmas" every year. The truth is, long before Black Friday sales and seasonal Starbucks cups, many Christians (yes, Christians) viewed Christmas as a thoroughly debauched and godless season. With all the raucous drinking, public carousing, and even violence, many reasoned that genuine Christians would never join in such immoral and irresponsible revelry. In addition, some of the symbols and rituals of Christmas seem disconnected from the true "reason for the season"; many are thought to be thoroughly pagan in origin. When you add to this sketchy history the fact that we don't know for certain when Jesus was born, sincere Christians might be tempted to discard Christmas observance entirely. What do we make of these concerns?

Let's start with the date of Jesus' birth. Despite various efforts to square our modern calendar with the historical event, no one knows for sure when Jesus was born. From the records we have, it seems the earliest Christians weren't very interested in determining the date. In the third century Clement of Alexandria writes that some calculated the day of the Lord's birth to be today's May 20 or April 20 or 21.[1] One hundred years later, in the mid-fourth century, we find widespread consensus building around two dates: December 25 in the West and January 6 or 7 in the East.

How did this happen? There are a few theories, but two are the most common. The best-known, especially in popular venues, is the "history of religions theory," which says December 25 was simply adopted from a pagan celebration. The Roman Empire celebrated a midwinter Saturnalia festival in late December, coinciding with the time of the winter solstice. And in 274 CE, the Feast of *Sol Invictus* (the Unconquered Sun) was formally established by Emperor Aurelian on December 25. So, the theory goes, early Christians intentionally seized on this coincidence to promote the Christian faith among pagans, claiming December 25 as Jesus' birthday.

The problem is that there is scant evidence for this view. Fourth-century Christian writers like Ambrose note the intersection of the winter solstice and Jesus' birth, but they don't speak of it as an intentional missional choice. In fact, it wasn't viewed as the church's choice at all. Instead, they saw the coincidence of the two dates as God's providential sign of Jesus' superiority over pagan gods. Jesus' birth on December 25, they said, proves that he is the true Sun who outshines all false gods.

The other problem with the Christians-adopting-a-pagan-holiday theory is that it is anachronistic. It attributes to the early church a practice that, up to that point, was foreign to them: intentionally assimilating pagan festivals into Christian ones. As a persecuted minority, Christians in the first three centuries were very concerned to distance themselves from pagan religious celebrations like temple sacrifices, games, and festivals. In fact, their refusal to participate in Roman religious devotion was one reason for their persecution. It would have gone against the grain of their practice at that point to purposely incorporate a pagan festival.

After the conversion of Emperor Constantine in 312 CE and the establishment of Christianity as the empire's favored religion, it became more common for Christian leaders to incorporate pagan festivals. We know Gregory the Great in the seventh century, for example, recommended his missionaries in modern-day Great Britain convert pagan temples into churches and transform pagan festivals into feasts for Christian martyrs. But the date of Christmas is very unlikely to have been chosen in this way, particularly since we know it is present in the historical record before Constantine's conversion.

The other theory about the dating of Christmas, often called the "calculation theory," has more going for it. The calculation theory says the dating of Christmas has to do with the dating of the annunciation (when the Virgin Mary was told she would be with child) and Jesus' conception, which was determined by dating Jesus' death at Passover. This can get a little complicated, especially given the difference in calendars between the Eastern and Western churches. But a brief summary goes like this: early church fathers determined that the date of Jesus' death (the fourteenth day of Nisan, according to the Gospel of John) in the year he died was equivalent to their March 25. Later the church recognized March 25 as the Feast of the Annunciation, which falls exactly nine months before December 25. So Jesus was thought to have been conceived and crucified on the same day of the year, with his birth occurring exactly nine months later.

Why would the church conclude that Jesus was conceived and killed on the same day? Some think it is rooted in ancient Jewish tradition about creation and redemption occurring in the same time of year. The Talmud, the central text of Rabbinic Judaism, reflects this point of view. For example, second-century Rabbi Yehoshua says, "In Nisan the world was created; in Nisan the Patriarchs were born; on Passover Isaac was born . . . and in Nisan in the future the Jewish people will be redeemed in the final redemption."[2] This reflects the expectation of a timely symmetry between human origins and human salvation. We have evidence of the same belief in an anonymous fourth-century Christian treatise from North Africa. And by the fifth century, Augustine was also familiar with the argument, saying, "For [Jesus] is believed to have been conceived on the 25th of March, upon which day also he suffered; so the womb of the Virgin, in which he was conceived, where no one of mortals was begotten, corresponds to the new grave in which he was buried, wherein was never man laid, neither before him nor since. But he was born, according to tradition, upon December the 25th."[3]

Scholars convinced of the calculation theory think the same logic is at work in the Eastern dating of Christmas. But instead of the fourteenth day of Nisan in the Hebrew calendar, the Greek fathers used the fourteenth day of the spring month in the Greek calendar, which is our April 6. April 6 is exactly nine months before January 6, which was originally the Eastern date for Christmas (beginning at sundown). As a result, Christians in the East and West calculated the date of Jesus' birth based on the belief that his death and conception took place on the same day, though due to their respective calendars, they came up with slightly different results.[4]

In the end, though, we must admit we don't know with certainty the exact date of Jesus' birth and likely never will. But I don't think it matters much—the point is, Jesus was born. He was born as a particular person in a particular time and place: a poor Jewish boy in Roman-occupied Judaea. "When the set time had fully come," Saint Paul says, "God sent his Son, born of a woman, born under the law, to redeem those under the law, that we might receive adoption to sonship" (Galatians 4:4-5).

From very early on the church has felt compelled to celebrate the birth of God's Son. And rightly so! It happens they chose a date on which to do so sometime in the fourth century. Though there is no empirically verifiable way to guarantee December 25 is *the day*, there's no good reason to refrain from celebrating the coming of Christ on that day either.

Unlike the contemporary retail-driven tendency to observe Christmas from the day after Thanksgiving through December 25, the Christmas season actually begins on Christmas Day. In 567 CE, the Council of Tours officially declared that the twelve days from Christmas Day to Epiphany ought to be observed as a sacred and festive season.[5] So before it became a jaunty song about exponentially multiplying gifts, the twelve days of Christmas referred to the time stretching from Christmas Day (December 25) through Epiphany (January 6).

In addition to the Feast of the Nativity (observed from sundown December 24 through December 25), the season of Christmas, or Christmastide, includes a number of other feasts and holy days as well: Saint Stephen's Day (December 26), the Feast of Saint John the Apostle (December 27), the Feast of the Holy Innocents (December 28), Saint

Sylvester's Day (New Year's Eve, December 31), the Feast of the Circumcision or Feast of the Holy Name (January 1), the Feast of the Holy Family (variable), and Twelfth Night (Epiphany Eve, January 5). Twelfth Night is the last night of the Christmas season, the day before the Feast of the Epiphany (January 6). We'll briefly discuss the significance of each of these days in the chapters that follow.

Viewed in themselves, these holy days aren't pagan in orientation. They were established to direct our hearts and minds to the story of Christ and his people—and to place our lives and communities within this sacred narrative. But there is more to the history. As Christianity spread out from the Middle East, becoming the established religion of Europe, the observance of Christmastide slowly evolved into a twelve-day spree of merriment and mischief-making. How these celebrations developed through the ages is a long and fascinating tale.[6] For our purposes, it helps to know that most of the population lived by agricultural rhythms. Since planting and harvesting were completed in spring, summer, and fall, wintertime coincided with the cessation of labor (including laying off seasonal workers) and slaughtering of livestock. Thus, winter was a natural time for relaxing, feasting, and, in the midst of widespread idleness, troublemaking. And it just so happens that all of this was taking place during Christmastide.

In the medieval period, especially, Christmas developed into a carnivalesque time for turning hierarchies and social conventions on their heads. Peasants went about demanding gifts from lords, threatening violence and looting if they weren't satisfied. (Remnants of this practice can still be heard in the lyrics to "We Wish You A Merry Christmas": "O, bring us some figgy pudding, And bring it right here! / We won't go until we get some, So bring it right here!") Servants dressed up as their masters and lampooned them publicly while men disguised themselves as women, parading through the streets drinking and caroling. Shakespeare's comedy *Twelfth Night* typifies the bawdy, upside-down nature of the festivities. A shipwrecked woman, Viola, pretends to be a man, creating an impossible comedic love triangle, and a pompous commoner, Malvolio, seeks to become a nobleman by marriage to one far beyond his station.

As you might imagine, the association of the twelve days of Christmas with partying, immorality, and social upheaval led many Christians during and after the Protestant

Reformation to forsake the holiday altogether. In fact, many used the supposed pagan origins of the December 25 date as one reason for denouncing the celebration. In the sixteenth century the English cleric Hugh Latimer had this to say: "Men dishonor Christ more in the twelve days of Christmas than in all the twelve months besides."[7] The Puritan party of the Church of England was especially outspoken, publishing tracts against Christmas and eventually outlawing it once they settled in New England. When you combine the association of Christmas with paganism and depravity, it begins to make sense why so many pious Protestants eschewed the holiday altogether.

With such strong opposition, how did Christmas make a comeback? There were many contributing social and cultural factors, including changes to the way Christmas was observed. In the nineteenth century Christmas shifted from a social and communal holiday to one focused on private hearth and home. This cut down significantly on vulgar public displays and increased spending among individual households. In this respect, the cultural influence of Clement Clarke Moore's "The Night Before Christmas" (1822) and Charles Dickens's *A Christmas Carol* (1834), both of which present a home-centered, generosity-focused Christmas, should not be underestimated. Whatever the confluence of factors, though, the bottom line is that by the late 1800s the average pew-sitting Protestant wanted to celebrate Christmas—and the clergy eventually complied. By the turn of the twentieth century, therefore, even the most virulently anti-Christmas groups, including the descendants of the Puritans, had finally embraced Christmastide festivities.[8]

What does all this history tell us? There's no doubt that some of the practices adopted during Christmastide have been immoral and unchristian. And Christians today should be discerning about how to observe the season so that the incarnation of God in Christ remains central rather than peripheral. But history does not support the premise that Christmas is pagan in origin. The date of Christmas was fixed by the fifth century and the church established the observance of the twelve days of Christmas in the sixth century.

The point of Christmas, like the rest of the liturgical calendar, is to attune our whole selves to the triune God. Observed with wisdom, thoughtfulness, and care, the twelve days of Christmas provide numerous opportunities to rejoice in God's salvific work in Christ and open ourselves to the Spirit's transforming power in our hearts, homes, and communities.

For Further Reading

Saint Augustine. *Sermons for Christmas and Epiphany*. Translated by Thomas Comerford Lawler. New York: Newman, 1952.

Marchand, Chris. *Celebrating the 12 Days of Christmas: A Guide for Churches and Families*. Eugene, OR: Wipf & Stock, 2019.

Nissenbaum, Stephen. *The Battle for Christmas: A Social and Cultural History of Our Most Cherished Holiday*. New York: Vintage, 1997.

2

God of the Great Exchange

The first Christmas my husband and I celebrated as a married couple took place in the home of my mother-in-law, Susan. I knew that Susan loved Christmas, but I wasn't prepared for the all-out extravaganza her ceaseless energy would produce. Her home was top-to-bottom holiday decorations, with Christmas lights everywhere possible and a large, tinsel-draped evergreen in the center of the living room. The tree was topped with a large LED star that changed colors on a timer, pink to purple to blue to green to yellow. The piano, tables, and every possible ledge were filled with decorations of all kinds: a ceramic holy family, reindeer figurines (with Rudolph leading the way), Winnie the Pooh and friends dressed for winter, snowmen and Santa Clauses, and scented candles of all kinds.

The energy of the decorations was rivaled only by Susan herself, who was filled with giddy joy at the prospect of having her family near and being able to give them the perfect gifts. It was all very charming until the morning of Christmas Day, when she knocked on our guest room door at four-thirty a.m., yelling in a singsong voice: "Wake up! Wake up! It's Christmas! Santa came! Time to open presents!"

Glaring groggily at my new husband, I whispered in a whine-growl, "Why is she waking us up so early?"

He grinned sheepishly and shrugged, "I don't know, honey. She just loves Christmas."

The undiluted delight on Susan's face as we opened presents was a sight I'll never forget. Her death to pancreatic cancer in 2006 left an unfillable hole in our holiday festivities. No one loved giving gifts as much as Susan.

While Christmas traditions vary the world over, gift-giving is a central practice just about anywhere Christ's birth is celebrated. Sometimes gifts are exchanged on December 6, the feast day of Saint Nicholas, and sometimes on Twelfth Night, the last day of Christmas, but most commonly on Christmas Eve or Christmas Day, the official liturgical start of the season. Many people look to the gifts of the Magi as the original inspiration for Christmas gift-giving. But how the Magi's gifts of gold, frankincense, and myrrh for the Christ child transformed into the gift-giving extravaganza Christmas has become is a long and complicated story. A few high points are worth noting.

Before the birth of Christ, gift-giving was common in the Roman Empire to mark the start of the New Year. When the date of the Christmas feast was set on December 25, it was situated closely to an established gift-giving occasion in the surrounding culture. It makes some sense, then, for the gift-giving practice to migrate to Christmas once the date was recognized.

Then, in the fourth century, Nicholas the bishop of Myra in Asia Minor became renowned for his sanctity and generosity, especially his gifts to poor families and children. One story has him dropping gold coins in a poor family's stockings while they dried by the hearth. Tradition says the reason for the gift was the provision of suitable dowries so the family's three daughters could marry. Due to his beloved memory, the day of Nicholas's death, December 6, became a traditional date of giving gifts to children in his honor. Many families leave out their shoes the night of December 5 so Saint Nicholas can fill them with sweets and small gifts overnight. Saint Nicholas is, of course, the historical basis for the myth of Santa Claus, popularized by Clement Clarke Moore's poem "A Visit from St. Nicholas / The Night Before Christmas" (1822) and clever retail advertising campaigns.

Beyond the Saint Nicholas tradition, gift-giving during the Christmas season was primarily communal until the late-modern period. Christmas plays, Saint Nicholas processions, and wassailing (or caroling) often included sharing gifts. In the spirit of the season, peasants and apprentices would demand treats and gifts from landowners, while servants received Christmas boxes for their efforts. Most of these gifts were meat, grains, fruit, and wine or ale—the literal fruits of their labor.

When Anglo-Saxon and German immigrants crossed the Atlantic, some of these traditions came with them. But, as we'd expect, the gift-giving ritual was slowly modified in its new environment. Two factors contributed to the change. First, society transformed from primarily agrarian to primarily industrial, which increased the ability of manufacturers to mass-produce consumer goods, lowering the cost of many things and making them more widely available. Industrialization also contributed to the movement of many people into cities, which created a new class system. As the middle class emerged, the nuclear family was romanticized as a peaceful haven from the industrialized and commercial city. Thus the home became the primary focus of the Christmas season with private gift-giving rituals (to children and other dependents) replacing public ones (to peasants, servants, and the like). Meanwhile, through European colonial rule and multiple waves of missionary efforts, Western Christians took their practices of Christmas gift-giving with them throughout the world. Today Christians on every continent exchange gifts for the Christmas holiday.

In the late nineteenth century in the United States, savvy retailers capitalized on the newly domesticated practice of Christmas gift-giving. Helped by the introduction of print catalogs and dependable mail service, department stores and toymakers began to market to parents and then directly to children. It worked, of course.[1] By the mid-twentieth century, the weeks leading up to Christmas had become the most profitable of the entire year—so much so that retailers now build their annual budgets around it. In the year 2018, retail spending reached its highest point ever with shoppers in the United States surpassing one trillion dollars (that's twelve zeros!)

in purchases during the Christmas season.[2] Certainly this is a far cry from the simple coins of Saint Nicholas!

It's easy to wrinkle our noses and look down on this glut of (often wasteful) spending. There is good reason to consider whether and how Christians ought to participate in the widespread consumption of the Christmas season. Personally, I find myself sympathetic with the complaint of C. B. Wheeler, who in 1904 was already lamenting rooms "glutted with a perfect shopful of toys" and spoiled, demanding children. He offered the possibility of creating an "Anti-gift League" in response.[3] I'm not sure the answer is to be anti-gift, but there's undoubtedly room for Christians to consider intentional, organized efforts to combat the consumerism surrounding Christmas. We need wisdom—and God will surely grant it if we ask (James 1:5).

Profligate shopping sprees and conspicuous consumption notwithstanding, the practice of gift-giving in itself remains evocative of the central mystery of Christmas: the incarnation of God in Christ. Christmas is about God's great gift to us, which is God's own self in the person of Jesus Christ. This reality is what one seasonal antiphon describes as *admirabile commercium*: the "great exchange" or "wonderful gift." Because of the great exchange of the incarnation, there's a sense in which every gift given, every box opened, contains an echo, however muddled, of the gift given by our Creator.

If the incarnation of God in Christ is the great exchange, then what, exactly, was exchanged? The antiphon summarizes beautifully the eternal reality of which our fallible gift-giving is an echo:

O wondrous exchange:
the Creator of humankind,
taking upon him a living body,
vouchsafed to be born of a Virgin
and, without seed, becoming a man,
hath made us partakers of his Divinity.[4]

God became human, the antiphon says. The Son exchanged the glories of divinity for unity with humankind. Then humans became one with God. Through the Son humanity exchanges sin and death for participation in the divine life. Saint Athanasius summarizes this two-part exchange with striking simplicity: "[The Word] became fully human so that we might become god."[5] Or, to put it another way, "The Word was humanized so that we might become divinized."

First, the Word became human. The first chapter of John's Gospel—a lectionary reading appointed for Christmas Day—explains this mystery in great detail. Rather than offer a genealogy or a narrative of Jesus' birth, John goes all the way back to the beginning (eternity past, so to speak), prior to the creation of the world. "In the beginning was the Word," John says, "and the Word was with God, and the Word was God. . . . The Word became flesh and made his dwelling among us. We have seen his glory, the glory of the one and only Son, who came from the Father, full of grace and truth" (John 1:1, 14).

"The Word" is a strange title to modern ears, but it would not have been strange to first-century listeners. For them "the word" (*ha logos* in Greek) was a common philosophical category referring to divine reason, wisdom, or self-expression.[6] John is telling his reader that the God who spoke creation into existence (Genesis 1:3) has spoken to creation finally and fully in Jesus Christ. Just as a person's words reveal what lies within their heart (for good or ill), so also the Word made flesh, Jesus Christ, reveals God in all of God's fullness. As the hymn "O Come, All Ye Faithful" says, "Word of the Father, now in flesh appearing / O come, let us adore him."

I like the way Eugene Peterson renders John 1:14 in *The Message*: "The Word became flesh and blood, and moved into the neighborhood." This says in colloquial language what Christians confess has happened theologically. The Word, God the Son, set aside the prerogatives of deity to become human and live among us. The one who existed in an eternal relationship of joyful, self-giving, loving communion of Father, Son, and Holy Spirit chose freely to unite himself to creation, human beings in particular, taking upon himself all the weakness and limitation such existence requires. In one of the earliest Christian hymns, Saint Paul says it this way:

> [Christ Jesus], being in very nature God,
>> did not consider equality with God something
>>> to be used to his own advantage;
> rather, he made himself nothing
>> by taking the very nature of a servant,
>> being made in human likeness. (Philippians 2:6-7)

God in human likeness. The enormity of this great exchange and its implications boggle the mind. Pastors and theologians throughout history have found themselves resorting to poetry and paradox to approach an explanation.

Saint Augustine says it memorably in one Christmas sermon: "The Maker of man became Man that he, Ruler of the stars, might be nourished at the breast; that he, the Bread, might be hungry; that he, the Fountain, might thirst; that he, the Light, might sleep."[7] Saint John Chrysostom was filled with similar awe as he sought to speak of the nativity:

> The Ancient of Days has become an infant. He who sits upon the sublime and heavenly throne now lies in a manger. And he who cannot be touched, who is without complexity, incorporeal, now lies subject to human hands. He who has broken the bonds of sinners is now bound by an infant's bands. But he has decreed that the ignominy shall become honor, infamy be clothed with glory, and abject humiliation the measure of his goodness. For this he assumed my body, that I may become capable of his word; taking my flesh, he gives me his spirit; and so he bestowing and I receiving, he prepares for me the treasure of life.[8]

O wondrous exchange, indeed! What kind of God is this? The New Testament declares that Jesus is "the image of the invisible God" (Colossians 1:15) and "the radiance of God's glory and the exact representation of his being" (Hebrews 1:3). Jesus says it even more simply: "Anyone who has seen me has seen the Father" (John 14:9). And what do we see when we behold the Word made flesh? We see God condescending to the limitations and indignities of the human condition. We see God demonstrating sovereign power through humble, self-sacrificing, and long-suffering love. We see the magnitude of God's glory precisely in the meekness of God's self-emptying. We see a God who deigns to move in next door, roll up his sleeves, and get dirt under his fingernails. This is one reason we dare not scoff at Christmas crèche displays, however dated, maudlin, or hackneyed they may seem. We know that to behold the face of the infant Jesus is to behold the face of our Creator.

So the Word became flesh, and we now confess that Jesus Christ is "God from God, Light from Light, true God from true God" (Nicene Creed). But there's still more to say. As we confess that Jesus Christ is fully divine, we also need to confess that he is fully human. The Word did not simply appear human or put on a human body, like someone putting on a suit of clothes. The Word became human in every way that we are human—except without sin. Thus, we confess that Jesus Christ is one person with two natures, divine and human. The fancy phrase the early church came up with for this reality is *hypostatic union*, which is a way to say that the divine and human natures of Christ are truly united—truly and eternally one—and that the divine and human natures remain fully divine and fully human even in the unity.

The great exchange—the truth of the incarnation at the heart of Christmas—requires a basic understanding of what Christians confess about the person of Christ. If the Word were only partially God, or a created demigod like Heracles or Perseus, then he could not unite humankind with God. And if the Word were only partially human, with a human body but not a human mind, for instance, or if he only appeared to be human, then he could not unite God to humankind. The great exchange requires all of God to be united to all of humankind for all eternity. That's why Christians confess that Jesus Christ is fully human and fully God, united in one person forever and ever.

We've considered what it means for the Word to become flesh. But what does it mean for humans to be divinized? The last line of the antiphon above says it this way: "[He] hath made us partakers of his Divinity." Yes, God became human in Christ. But it goes the other way, too: in Christ human beings are united to God. Just as the Godhead condescended to be united to humankind forever in Jesus Christ, so also humankind has ascended in Jesus Christ to be united to the Godhead forever. In his very own person the God-man has made the way for us to become participants in the divine life or "partakers of the divine nature" (2 Peter 1:4 NKJV). Through Christ human beings exchange death for life, sin for righteousness, mortality for immortality. The Christmas liturgy of the Catholic Church says it this way:

> For through [Christ] the holy exchange that
>   restores our life
> has shone forth today in splendor:
> when our frailty is assumed by your Word
> not only does human mortality receive unending
>   honor
> but by this wondrous union we, too, are made
>   eternal.[9]

Early church fathers compared divinization to the burning bush in Exodus 3 or to the behavior of iron placed into fire. The bush Moses encountered on Mount Horeb was aflame with the presence of God but not consumed by it. That is, the bush did not cease to be a bush, nor was the bush destroyed by God's presence. Rather, it became a bush in an incomparably glorious form—ablaze with uncreated divine glory. An iron placed into the fire functions similarly. On its own, the iron is hard, cold, and unchanging. But after being immersed in burning coals the iron takes on the qualities of fire—searing hot and glowing red. The iron does not cease to be iron, but now it is iron in a superlative way—iron suffused with fire. So it is with human beings who are joined to God in Christ. We do not cease to be human, nor is our humanity destroyed through union with God. Rather we become more fully human in an extraordinarily elevated manner— immersed body and soul in the beauty and glory of God.

None of this means the essential difference between God and humankind is done away with. God remains uncreated and humans remain created. In fact, it is precisely because God is God that he is able to enter our condition and rescue us from the powers of darkness without being overcome by them. But the astonishing truth remains: God has seen fit to give us the gift of sharing in God's own life, to be united with God forever. The ambition of Adam and Eve in the Garden of Eden was that they would be like God (Genesis 3:5-6). Now, as Benedict XVI says, that desire is fulfilled in Christ but in a wholly unexpected way. In God's self-emptying, God comes down, joins us to himself, and "raises us to the true greatness of his being."[10]

The great exchange comes about purely by God's gracious initiative. God's original creation of the world was sheer gift, for the triune God had no need to fill or problem to solve. God's re-creation of the world in the incarnation is sheer gift, too. It is certainly not through human efforts, which avail nothing. In our disobedience we had become subject to evil, sin, and death, and God in his mercy initiated a rescue mission in the incarnation. In the great exchange we remember that human beings are raised to a status even more exalted than we had at creation's beginning: united with the life of the triune God forever.

Our gift-giving at Christmas will always fall short of the glory of the great exchange. The adults in my family often joke about "winning Christmas" with the gifts we choose for each other. As presents are opened, the most appropriate and swoon-worthy gift is declared the "winner." Usually it's the one that causes the recipient to cry with tears of joy. I think my personal favorite was the year our family had special portraits taken and got them printed on a blanket for my mom. The kids' smiling faces quickly got the waterworks going, and we officially "won" Christmas that year.

In rural Msinga, a municipality in the KwaZulu-Natal province of South Africa, the highlight of Christmas Day festivities is when men, newly returned home from work in the big cities, gather to sing and dance. In call-and-response melodies, accompanied by energetic dancing, the men sing playfully of the holiday gifts they are expected to bring their families. "The plane I've bought for my darling is coming," they sing. "You'll get your stove this afternoon / not a coal one, darling, but a gas one. . . . The [temperature] setting will be just right."[11] Amid the joy of returning home to family and friends, they humorously express the very real pressure of being able to provide the right gifts.

My family's running gag and the Msinga men's songs are in good-natured fun. But both highlight the fact that humans give gifts for a variety of not-so-noble reasons: as an effort to outdo others, in a bid to manipulate, as an attempt to assuage guilt, or out of a sense of obligation. In our best moments, though, we give gifts as tangible expressions of love—not sentimental, soft-focused love, but clear-eyed, knowledgeable, active love. To love another is to will their good. Gift-giving, then, is best practiced as an expression of this goodwill. And when done in this way, Christmas presents can, in a very small way, demonstrate the great exchange—the ultimate expression of love that lies at the heart of new creation in Christ.

Of course, gift-giving is not the only way to acknowledge the great exchange at Christmas. Historically, four masses (or liturgies) are held between Christmas Eve and Christmas Day: one during the day on Christmas Eve and three more from sundown Christmas Eve through Christmas Day morning.[12] Many churches today opt for only two services: one on Christmas Eve (sometimes called Midnight Mass) and one on Christmas Day. And some worship only on Christmas Eve, leaving Christmas Day for families. Regardless of the timing, it is essential for Christians to set aside time for corporate worship and give thanks together for the great exchange.

Indeed, one way to "keep Christ in Christmas" is to "keep the Mass in Christmas." Not only is God worthy of our worship, but God has promised to meet us when we gather to worship and pray. Marking Christmas Eve and

Christmas Day with communal worship allows us to begin the twelve days of Christmas with the proper focus: the God of the great exchange. One of three Anglican collects appointed for Christmas Day highlights the gift of God and our hope for God's transforming work in us:

> Almighty God, you have given your only-begotten Son to take our nature upon him, and to be born this day of a pure virgin: Grant that we, who have been born again and made your children by adoption and grace, may daily be renewed by your Holy Spirit; through our Lord Jesus Christ, to whom with you and the same Spirit be honor and glory, now and forever. Amen.[13]

According to the Italian legend of La Befana, the elderly Befana was visited by the Magi a few days before the birth of Christ. They requested directions to where the child was, but Befana did not know. She offered them hospitality for the night and they stayed with her. The Magi spent the evening telling of the star they had followed from the East, eventually inviting Befana to join their journey to find the Messiah. But preoccupied by her housework and other duties, Befana declined and remained behind. As time passed, though, Befana realized the foolishness of her decision. She packed a bag full of gifts and set out with haste to find the Magi. But they had already traveled beyond her reach. So Befana sought the infant Jesus on her own, night after night, trying to make her way to Bethlehem.

Legend says Befana was never able to find the Magi or the Christ child and she has continued her search through the centuries to this very day. Every year, on the eve of the Epiphany, she leaves children gifts of toys, candy, and fruit, hoping somehow, some way, to find and honor the Christ child.

If we are to avoid Befana's fate of defaulting to holiday busyness and missing the Christ child, we must prioritize the liturgical journey to Christmas through communal worship. Yes, church attendance on Christmas Day requires rearranging schedules, including gift-opening and household meals. Yes, organizing worship for Christmas Eve and Christmas Day requires more of clergy, musicians, and volunteers. But amid the consumerism threatening to overwhelm the Christmas season, corporate worship is the best way to pursue the renewal by the Holy Spirit we all desperately need.

What better embodiment of the Feast of the Incarnation could there be than standing before God, in the company of God's people, with hands open and outstretched to receive the gift of God's own self in the flesh and blood of Christ? With our festivities properly framed in the worship of the Word made flesh, our gift exchanges will speak more clearly of the great exchange God has undertaken on our behalf.

FOR FURTHER READING

St. Athanasius. *On the Incarnation.* Translated by John Behr. Popular Patristics Series. Yonkers, NY: St. Vladimir's Seminary Press, 2012.

DePaola, Tomie. *The Legend of Old Befana.* New York: Simon & Schuster, 2017.

English, Adam C. *The Saint Who Would Be Santa Claus: The True Life and Trials of Nicholas of Myra.* Waco, TX: Baylor University Press, 2012.

3

God of the Poor

When my three children were small, we experienced an especially memorable Christmas Eve service. Our youngest, almost two years old at the time, fell asleep soundly on the drive to church. I have a photo of her from that night, cradled against my husband's chest, cherubic face and golden hair framed in his strong arms. I still remember how the sight of her asleep against the backdrop of twinkling decorations and joyous Christmas hymns made me sigh with contented happiness.

Near the end of the service, though, the slumbering angel awoke grumpy and demanding. She nearly set her hair on fire with the candle she insisted on holding herself. Only her dad's quick thinking averted disaster, and he accidentally burned his own arm instead. What goes well with "Silent Night" sung by candlelight? The smell of singed arm hair, of course.

I have often thought how much easier worship services would be without the unpredictable dynamism children bring with them. I'm sure other parents and caregivers can relate. But there's no doubt the ease would be far outweighed by the loss. Children are beloved of God and special recipients of God's kingdom. We lose something important when they aren't with us. In fact, children are among those people with whom Jesus so closely identifies that they become a sacramental sign. The hungry, the thirsty, the stranger, the unclothed, the sick, the imprisoned, children—Jesus says of all these that to welcome and serve them is to welcome and serve him (see Matthew 18:5; 25:40; Mark 9:37). So we separate ourselves from the poor, needy, and vulnerable at our collective peril.

Every Christmas, Christians in the Philippines practice welcoming the poor and the stranger through a pageant called *Panunulúyan*. It is modeled after the Spanish tradition of *Las Posadas* (literally, "The Inns"), a dramatic procession attributed to Saint John of the Cross from the sixteenth century. Both *Las Posadas* and *Panunulúyan* feature a procession that reenacts Joseph and Mary's journey from Nazareth to Bethlehem, especially their search for lodging upon arrival. Performed after dark, singers process through town following people who are holding aloft images or statues of Mary and Joseph. They visit house after house (chosen in advance), chanting a song meant to incite the homeowners, played by a choir, to let the holy family stay. Over and over the homeowners cruelly turn the weary travelers away.

Finally, as midnight approaches, Mary and Joseph find their way to the parish church, where a replica of the nativity has been erected. The birth of Jesus is celebrated at midnight with the *Simbang Gabi*, or *Misa de Gallo*, the Christmas Eve Mass. Traditionally the processing singers use lanterns, called *paróls*, fashioned in the shape of a star representing the star of Bethlehem. Today, brightly colored star-shaped lanterns are used to decorate homes and are one of the most iconic symbols of Filipino Christmas.

The Philippines has a long history of both deep Christian faith and fierce resistance to colonial oppression. So it makes sense that a tradition like the *Panunulúyan*, which foregrounds both the holy family's search for refuge and the practice of hospitality, remains vital for Filipino Christmastide. They know God is love, and, as the Tagalog carol "Ang Pasko ay Sumapit" ("Christmas Is Here") says,

> Let us all sing
> While the world is quiet.
> Now comes the day
> Of the Child sent by heaven.
> Let us love each other.
> Let us follow the golden rule.
> And starting now
> Even if it is not Christmas
> Let us give to each other.[1]

The mystery of the incarnation is, in Gustavo Gutiérrez's words, "an incarnation into littleness"—transcendent power taking on mortal weakness amid a violent world. The Word of God appears among us as a helpless child smelling of the stable.[2] When it comes to Christmas, then, children (even irritable, uncooperative ones), as well as all those lowly and in need, point us toward one of Christmas's and Scripture's central themes: God's love for the vulnerable, weak, and poor.

For many Christians around the world, God's love for the vulnerable is embodied at Christmas through charitable service and giving to those in need. Of course, this ought not be the only time of year when Christians serve and give to the poor, but traditionally it has been highlighted in a distinctive way. Saint Stephen's Day, or the Feast of Saint Stephen (December 26), also called Boxing Day, has special significance in this regard. Saint Stephen was the church's first deacon, chosen to serve the poor because of his exemplary faith and Spirit-filled life (Acts 6:5). He was also the church's first martyr (Acts 6:8–7:60), and he died praying for the forgiveness of his killers, as Christ himself did (Acts 7:60).

Because of Stephen's service to the poor and courageous martyrdom, the church has commemorated Saint Stephen's Day since at least the fifth century. Through his witness we remember that all Christians are called to serve those in need and lay down our lives for others. As Chris Marchand says, "Bound up in December 26, right after having celebrated the birth of Christ, there is a reminder that we are to take up our crosses and follow him, that our glory is in humble obedience and servant-hearted love toward others."[3]

Since at least the Middle Ages, Saint Stephen's Day has been observed as a special day for giving to the poor. Many churches throughout Europe had special offering boxes near the entrance where worshipers could offer alms to the parish's poor. The day after Christmas, in memory of Saint Stephen, the priest would open the box and distribute the contents to those who needed it most. It was also customary for landowners to give gifts to those who worked in their household and labored on their lands. Sometimes these gifts were bestowed spontaneously during times of Christmastide wassailing. Sometimes they were given through formal Christmas boxes filled with various wares from the landowner's property (hence, "Boxing Day"). In the late eighteenth and early nineteenth centuries, it became common for the higher classes to organize charitable events to raise money for various causes, many of which involved children.

Not all these charitable activities were offered in the spirit of Christian love and generosity—and the same is true in our day. Nevertheless, the practice of sacrificial giving around the Christmas season is an outworking of the church's teaching that to give to those in need is to give to Jesus himself. As Martin Luther says in a Christmas sermon, "He who gives of his goods to help the poor, to send children to school, to educate them in God's Word and other arts . . . he is giving to the baby Jesus."[4]

Moreover, the church has taught since the Middle Ages that giving to the poor is one of the corporal (that is, bodily) works of mercy, which includes feeding the hungry, giving drink to the thirsty, clothing the naked, sheltering the homeless, visiting the sick, ransoming the imprisoned, and burying the dead.[5] All these acts are practices by which Christians demonstrate love for God and neighbor (see Matthew 22:37-40) and grow in the virtue of mercy.

The tradition of Saint Stephen's Day is referenced in the popular Christmas carol "Good King Wenceslas," written in the nineteenth century by John Mason Neale. The lyrics relate the tale of a tenth-century Bohemian ruler, Wenceslas, who would later become the patron saint of the Czech people. Looking out his window on Saint Stephen's Day, the song says, Wenceslas sees a poor peasant gathering wood in the cold snow. The good king is moved to act and enlists his page's help to bless the needy man and his family with rich food, drink, and wood logs for their hearth.

> Page and monarch, forth they went,
>   forth they went together;
> Through the rude wind's wild lament
>   and the bitter weather.

Though the page falters in the snowy, frigid night, Wenceslas urges him on, telling him to follow carefully in his own footsteps. The boy soldiers on, finding that his master's footprints are inexplicably warm, presumably a result of the saint's warm, generous heart. The final verse exhorts the listener:

> Therefore, Christian men, be sure,
> wealth or rank possessing,
> Ye who now will bless the poor,
> shall yourselves find blessing.

Sharing what we have and caring for the poor has been Christian practice since the earliest days of the church. The book of Acts reports that the first Christians "were together and had everything in common. They sold property and possessions to give to anyone who had need" (Acts 2:44-45). This generosity paid off, apparently, because Acts reports later, "There were no needy persons among them" (Acts 4:34).

We know from the letters of Saint Paul that he collected money to distribute to poor believers (1 Corinthians 16:1-4; 2 Corinthians 8:1-15), and Saints James and John emphasize in their Epistles the Christian's obligation to provide for others' bodily needs as an expression of faith and love (James 2:1-26; 1 John 3:11-24). Indeed, it is the perspective of the New Testament that the "haves" need to give their wealth away just as much as the "have-nots" need to receive it. Jesus says plainly, "It is hard for someone who is rich to enter the kingdom of heaven" (Matthew 19:23). Through practices of giving we learn not to rely on earthly treasures for security and provision but on the Lord.

The Christian emphasis on works of mercy doesn't rule out addressing the social and political factors that lead to inequality, poverty, and the like. Christians ought not divorce mercy from justice or charitable efforts from social activism. As we devote ourselves to the work of bandaging up the wounded, so to speak, we should also ask how they were wounded in the first place. It is faithful Christian service both to care for the victim of robbery on the road to Jericho and also to work to reduce or eliminate robbery on the road to Jericho. Both are necessary, and both are an outworking of God's love for the poor.

Among the accounts of Jesus' birth, Luke's Gospel seems to highlight most clearly the honored place of the vulnerable in God's story of redemption. Luke describes the annunciation this way: "In the sixth month of Elizabeth's pregnancy, God sent the angel Gabriel to Nazareth, a town in Galilee, to a virgin pledged to be married to a man named Joseph, a descendant of David. The virgin's name was Mary. The angel went to her and said, 'Greetings, you who are highly favored! The Lord is with you'" (Luke 1:26-28). Who is the Lord with? Mary, an unknown Jewish peasant woman living in a remote town on the outskirts of the Roman Empire. Her people have suffered under pagan rule for about five hundred years and now find themselves dominated by the most powerful empire of the age. They have maintained faith and faithfulness to God but at great cost. Still, the Lord comes to Mary and invites her to join him in the salvation of the world. The angel continues:

> Do not be afraid, Mary; you have found favor with God. You will conceive and give birth to a son, and you are to call him Jesus. He will be great and will be called the Son of the Most High. The Lord God will give him the throne of his father David, and he will reign over Jacob's descendants forever; his kingdom will never end. (Luke 1:30-33)

Mary is understandably puzzled and asks how this will happen since she is yet unmarried. The angel assures her, "The Holy Spirit will come on you, and the power of the Most High will overshadow you. So the holy one to be born will be called the Son of God" (Luke 1:35). As a sign of God's power, Gabriel tells Mary of her cousin Elizabeth, who is now six months pregnant despite being presumed barren: "For no word from God will ever fail" (Luke 1:37).

Mary's response to God's invitation is an unreserved *yes*: "I am the Lord's servant. . . . May your word to me be fulfilled" (Luke 1:38). The significance of Mary's assent can't be overstated. Her *yes*, grace-filled and God-gifted, is truly cosmos-shaking. In this moment she becomes God's willing covenant partner in the restoration of all creation. Mary's *yes* changes literally everything, and she sets the example for all who come after her: the first and exemplary disciple in the community of Jesus' disciples.

Countless artists have attempted to capture the wonder of Mary's encounter with Gabriel, but none in my view have done so as beautifully as Henry Ossawa Tanner in *The Annunciation* (1898), which currently hangs in the Philadelphia Museum of Art. Son of an African Methodist Episcopal minister, Tanner specialized in painting

Christian subjects. In 1897 he traveled to Egypt and Palestine in order to experience the people, architecture, and culture of the Holy Land. Upon his return he painted the moment the angel appears to Mary, drawing on insights gleaned during his trip.

In Tanner's composition Mary is depicted as a black-haired peasant girl, seated sideways on her bed as if awakened in the middle of the night. Within the small chamber a woven striped rug lies across the stone ground and a dark red and orange covering hangs behind her (perhaps the colors of her clan). She is barefoot and dressed in rumpled striped robes, her hands folded humbly in her lap. Her face and eyes are upturned, illuminated by the only light in the room: a pillar of golden light hovering at the edge of the scene. Tanner's Gabriel has no wings or halo or even a recognizable physical form. He is a wondrous light illuminating the darkness of her chamber. And Mary wears no mark of celestial saintliness either— Tanner opts to emphasize instead the unassuming humanness of Mary, daughter of a modest first-century Jewish family.

Tanner's painting helps us better understand the quiet profundity of the moment when Mary responds to

Gabriel's invitation. In the stillness of the night, no one beyond the walls of her bedchamber knows a world-transforming event is taking place: heaven and earth coming together in an entirely new way. In the sweeping story of Scripture, Mary's assent to God is the redemptive recapitulation of Eve's *yes* to the serpent. And through her *yes*, Mary will become the living tabernacle for God's presence. Just as the glory of God overshadowed the tabernacle and the ark within it (Exodus 40:34), so the Spirit of God overshadows Mary (Luke 1:35). And just as David leaped with joy in the presence of the ark of the covenant (2 Samuel 6:14), so also John the Baptist in Elizabeth's womb will leap with joy in the presence of Mary, Mother of the Lord (Luke 1:44). A peasant woman has become the living ark of the new covenant, filled with the Holy Spirit and bearing the Son of God in her womb. "There is such richness and goodness in this Nativity," Martin Luther says, "that if we should see and deeply understand, we should be dissolved in perpetual joy."[6]

After her encounter with Gabriel, Mary bears her holy treasure to the hill country of Judea. There she spends three months with her cousin Elizabeth, who is preparing for her own miraculous birth. At their first encounter,

Mary proclaims the greatness of God in song, a passage often called the Magnificat (from the first word of the song in the Latin translation). The Word conceived in her flesh now inspires her with words of prophetic praise. Mary declares that the mighty one has "been mindful of the humble state of his servant" and that "all generations" will call her blessed (Luke 1:48). The Lord doesn't act only for her, though. Mary's prophecy declares the powerful works of God on behalf of her suffering people:

> [God] has performed mighty deeds with his arm;
>> he has scattered those who are proud in their
>>> inmost thoughts.
> He has brought down rulers from their thrones
>> but has lifted up the humble.
> He has filled the hungry with good things
>> but has sent the rich away empty.
> He has helped his servant Israel,
>> remembering to be merciful
> to Abraham and his descendants forever,
>> just as he promised our ancestors. (Luke 1:51-55)

While the eyes of the world are on the powerful and mighty, Mary says, the eyes of the Lord are on the lowly and vulnerable. Indeed, Jean-Marc Éla says the incarnation "establishes a form of conspiracy between God and the downtrodden."[7] The lowly and the hungry become God's covenant collaborators in the re-creation of the cosmos.

Mary can testify to the power, goodness, and mercy of God because she is the recipient of a story going back hundreds of years. The God she proclaims is the God of Abraham, Isaac, and Jacob—the God of Sarah, Rebekah, and Leah. This God made a covenant with nomadic shepherds in Mesopotamia, calling them away from the myriad gods surrounding them to serve Yahweh alone. This God rescued the descendants of Abraham from slavery in Egypt, established an everlasting covenant with them at Mount Sinai, formed them into a nation through the law, and prospered them in a land not their own. Despite their repeated disobedience, an unfaithful monarchy, foreign conquests, exile, return, and additional conquests, this God continued to seek his people and work for their good. Because of this heritage, passed down from generation to generation, Mary knows she is poised at the beginning of the fulfillment of God's promises to Israel. The Son she carries embodies the mercy and faithfulness of God.

Mary's prophecy is echoed by Zechariah, Elizabeth's husband and John the Baptist's father, later in the same chapter. This text is traditionally called the Benedictus, and it shares themes with the Magnificat. Following the birth and naming of John, Zechariah too breaks forth in song:

> Praise be to the Lord, the God of Israel,
>> because he has come to his people and
>>> redeemed them.
> He has raised up a horn of salvation for us
>> in the house of his servant David
> (as he said through his holy prophets of long ago),
> salvation from our enemies
>> and from the hand of all who hate us—
> to show mercy to our ancestors
>> and to remember his holy covenant.
>> (Luke 1:68-72)

Within the story of God's dealings with Israel, the prophetic words of Mary and Zechariah demonstrate a profound truth: God delights in raising up the small and weak for special honor and glory. As Saint Paul says in his first letter to the Corinthians, "God chose the foolish things of the world to shame the wise; God chose the weak things of the world to shame the strong. God chose the lowly things of this world and the despised things—and the things that are not—to nullify the things that are, so that no one may boast before him" (1 Corinthians 1:27-29). The Savior of the world is born to a no-name peasant family in an insignificant community on the edge of the empire. And it is out of this life of obscurity among the working class of Galilee that Mary's Son will emerge to inaugurate God's kingdom of love and justice—a reality he learned as a boy from her words and example.

God's love for the vulnerable is illustrated well in the beloved animated film *Charlie Brown's Christmas*. Who can forget the climactic moment when Linus with his stocking cap and blanket walks to the spotlight and re-cites a portion of Luke's Gospel to explain the meaning of Christmas? But it's the arc of the entire story that demon-strates God's love so beautifully. Charlie Brown chooses the ugliest, most bedraggled tree for the Christmas play, to the chagrin of his peers. We might say Charlie Brown leaves the ninety-nine beautiful trees for the one lost and downtrodden tree.

But as the story progresses, Chuck's instincts are proved correct. The ugly tree is made lovely by being beloved; the lowliest tree is made glorious by being chosen and set apart. I'll admit I didn't understand the point of this story as a child. I found the whole thing rather baffling, to be honest. But now I see the deep Christian wisdom in the cartoon. In Charlie Brown's insistence on choosing the detestable tree to adopt and adorn, we get a small but vivid glimpse of God's compassion for the overlooked and forgotten.

Luke's version of the nativity, which Linus quotes so movingly, further elaborates on this theme. In Luke 2, Joseph and Mary are forced to leave their hometown due to the emperor's desire for a census of the empire. "So Joseph also went up from the town of Nazareth in Galilee to Judea, to Bethlehem the town of David, because he belonged to the house and line of David. He went there to register with Mary, who was pledged to be married to him and was expecting a child" (Luke 2:4-5).

The contrast couldn't be starker. While the world's most powerful man, who presumed to call himself savior and lord, forced his populace to disperse across the empire, the world's true Savior and Lord emerged from the womb of a Jewish peasant woman in a tiny town on the empire's margins. When the time of delivery arrived, the text says, "she gave birth to her firstborn, a son. She wrapped him in cloths and placed him in a manger" (Luke 2:7). Thus, the holy child is born into obscurity, brought forth in a room meant for livestock, and bound in wrappings evocative of grave clothes.

American poet Luci Shaw captures the enormity of this moment in her poem "Made Flesh":

After
The white-hot beam of annunciation
fused heaven with dark earth,
his searing, sharply focused light
went out for a while,
eclipsed in amniotic gloom:
his cool immensity of splendor,
his universal grace,
small-folded in a warm, dim
female space—
the Word stern-sentenced to be
nine months' dumb—
infinity walled in a womb,
until the next enormity—
the Mighty One, after submission
to a woman's pains,

helpless on a barn's bare floor,
first-tasting bitter earth.[8]

Who are the first to hear of the holy child's birth? Not the high priest's family, the regional aristocrats, or the imperial household, but "shepherds living out in the fields nearby, keeping watch over their flocks at night" (Luke 2:8). The shepherds represent the poor of Israel, "the simple souls whom Jesus would bless, because to them above all is granted access to the mystery of God."[9] These unnamed shepherds are given the experience of their lives: "An angel of the Lord appeared to them, and the glory of the Lord shone around them, and they were terrified" (Luke 2:9). As well they should be! They were settling down to their usual nightly routine and suddenly the God of their fathers revealed himself through a resplendent messenger.

God's angel speaks comfort and good news: "Do not be afraid. I bring you good news that will cause great joy for all the people. Today in the town of David a Savior has been born to you; he is the Messiah, the Lord. This will be a sign to you: You will find a baby wrapped in cloths and lying in a manger" (Luke 2:10-12). The "sign" could not be more unusual: a swaddled infant resting in a feeding trough. But let's not miss the full significance of the angel's words. The good news of great joy is for "all the people." *All* the people. And the Messiah-Lord is born in a first-century town with a particular history among a peculiar people—the descendants of Abraham, Moses, and David. Thus, the universal liberator of all nations comes to us through the particularity of a powerless and marginalized nation.

As if to confirm the trustworthiness of the angel's message, an angelic army appears to the shepherds as backup:

> Suddenly a great company of the heavenly host appeared with the angel, praising God and saying,
>
> > "Glory to God in the highest heaven,
> > > and on earth peace to those on whom his
> > > favor rests." (Luke 2:13-14)

The text says they are "saying" these things, but the church has often understood these words to have been sung. So Christians have sung the Gloria, which is based on the angelic proclamation, every Sunday (except during penitential seasons) for hundreds of years:

> Glory to God in the highest,
> and peace to his people on earth.
> Lord God, heavenly King,

almighty God and Father,

we worship you, we give you thanks,

we praise you for your glory.

The words again declare the universality of God's mission: God is glorified above, and the earth below is blessed by God's favor and good pleasure. And God's universal favor and good pleasure are manifested especially in the arrival of the Messiah in the little town of Bethlehem. Within the angels' message, Saint Bernard of Clairvaux hears a word of special consolation to the afflicted and poor of the world:

> It is to these, not to others, that the holy angels whisper consolation. It is to the shepherds, watching and keeping the night watches over their flocks, that the joy of the new light is announced. To them it is revealed that the Savior is born. Yes, to the poor, to the hard-working, not to the rich, who have their consolation here below. It is to the poor that the light of a glorious day has shone forth amid their vigils, and the night shall be light as the day.[10]

When the angels depart, the shepherds leave at once for Bethlehem. They find the holy family and the child in the manger, just as the angels said. The shepherds tell their extraordinary tale, to the amazement of Mary and Joseph, and then return to their flocks, "glorifying and praising God for all the things they had heard and seen, which were just as they had been told" (Luke 2:20). What had they seen and heard? The God of their fathers, the God of Sarah, Rebekah, and Leah, has come to his people at last—to dwell among them, save them, and bring the world to its future glory. And God discloses this universal mission first to the nameless shepherds watching their flocks by night.

Mary and the shepherds are precisely the lowly whom God delights in raising up for special honor. We recall this when we observe Saint Stephen's Day or other kinds of Christmas season giving. Giving is a practice crucial to our formation as people of generosity and self-forget-fulness. But there is something good and right about being particularly attentive to the needs of the poor during the Christmas season too. After all, it is the time in the church calendar when we recall the young Jewish woman whom God chose to bear the Word and become his covenant partner for the world's restoration. Christians who gather to celebrate the incarnation have seen, in the words of Dietrich Bonhoeffer, "the presence of God in the shape of a human child," and it has changed forever the way we perceive the small, weak, and powerless.[11] God's special love for the vulnerable and marginalized leads God's people to love them too.

It can be tricky to talk about wealth and poverty in the contemporary world. On the one hand, those in wealthy societies like the United States are increasingly aware of the disparity between our very high standard of living and the majority of the global population. Many Christians find themselves scandalized by the degree to which their relatively comfortable lives seem to be built on the unjust treatment and deprivation of people in other parts of the world. Lacking the power to do much about these global realities, Christians struggle to know what faithfulness to Jesus requires. Even within affluent countries, significant numbers of people lack the basic necessities of life. After all, the opposite of poverty is not wealth but enough. The poor are those who don't have enough food and clean water, shelter and physical safety, medical care, and the like. Given the economic precariousness of late-modern capitalism, even those living in affluent areas can find themselves in situations where they are no longer able to meet basic needs. During Christmastide, followers of Jesus are reminded of their special obligation to care for those who lack "enough."

At the same time, Christians know that material neediness isn't the only kind of poverty. There is also poverty of virtue; scarcity of faith, hope, and love; and destitution of spirit that can plague human beings regardless of their material conditions. This is not to undermine the seriousness with which we should take the material needs of people, but it is to acknowledge that modern life, with all of its benefits and luxuries, has also brought with it an extraordinary prevalence of spiritual poverty. Possessing the latest consumer goods by no means ensures participation in the good life. And elevated socioeconomic status does not protect us from leading selfish, vice-ridden, and vacuous lives. In fact, the New Testament suggests that the former actually makes the latter more likely. Saint Paul's words to Timothy seem particularly apt: "Those who want to get rich fall into temptation and a trap and into many foolish and harmful desires that plunge people into ruin and destruction. For the love of money is a root of all kinds of evil. Some people, eager for money, have wandered from the faith and pierced themselves with many griefs" (1 Timothy 6:9-10).

What are we to glean from all this in the Christmas season? Ultimately, those to whom Jesus comes in lowliness and great humility are those who acknowledge their need for him: "I have not come to call the righteous, but sinners to repentance" (Luke 5:32). At the same time, God has special affection for those in material need. So those whom God has called to repentance are also called to demonstrate their allegiance to Christ by giving away their possessions. In light of the dangers of riches for the soul, the wealthy need to make it a regular practice to give away their wealth—and the poor need the wealthy to give away their wealth to supply what they lack. It is a mutuality of giving and receiving, as Paul says: "Your plenty will supply what they need, so that in turn their plenty will supply what you need" (2 Corinthians 8:14). At Christmastime, therefore, in obedience to Christ, we give sacrificially, praying with the collect for the first Sunday after Christmas Day:

> Almighty God, you have poured upon us the new
> light of your incarnate Word: Grant that this light,
> enkindled in our hearts, may shine forth in our lives;

through Jesus Christ our Lord, who lives and reigns with you, in the unity of the Holy Spirit, one God, now and forever. Amen.

FOR FURTHER READING

Bonhoeffer, Dietrich. *The Mystery of the Holy Night*. New York: Crossroad, 1997.

Luther, Martin. *Martin Luther's Christmas Book*. Edited by Roland H. Bainton. Minneapolis: Fortress Press, 2017.

Shaw, Luci. *Accompanied by Angels: Poems of the Incarnation*. Grand Rapids, MI: Eerdmans, 2006.

4

God of Creation and Re-Creation

Some of my most vivid Christmas memories involve putting up and taking down decorations. My family never hung lights on the outside of the house, but we went all-out inside. Pre-lit garlands over the mantle, holly garlands around first-floor windows, wreaths on the doors, scented candles, decorative nutcrackers and Santa Clauses, stockings over the fireplace, crocheted pillows and throws, and, of course, a large Christmas tree sparkling with its own decorations. Getting everything out of the boxes and hung up was an all-day endeavor, as was the process of taking everything down. But the takedown process was complicated every year by the passionate protests of my younger sister.

Ten years my junior, Leah was desperately attached to our Christmas decor. For much of her childhood, the day we took down decorations was a harrowing event marked by her tearful tantrums. She never could articulate *why* she was so upset by the de-decorating process—she was a young child, after all—but she made it clear she didn't want it to go. Now that I'm an adult with my own children, I think I understand. Christmas decorations take the ordinary aspects of our lives and make them extraordinary. With some greenery, glass ornaments, and miniature lights, we can make our humdrum living room into a charming, picturesque space. After several weeks of enjoying such beauty, along with the family togetherness and special events the beauty signaled, my sister didn't want to go back to normal. She wanted to hold on to the enchantment for just a little bit longer.

The cynical among us will point out that, beautiful as they are, Christmas decorations are part of the commercialization and consumerism of the Christmas season. It's a fair point. Christmas decorations are big business, especially in the United States. Most of us can't imagine Christmas without some kind of decoration—and we're willing to spend good money on it. But when the twelve days of Christmas were established as a liturgical holiday, there were no Christmas trees or twinkling lights. So where does the now-ubiquitous practice of Christmas trees and holiday decorations come from?

Though many in the modern period have sought to trace the Christmas tree back to pre-Christian paganism, historians now acknowledge this is a myth. Others have attempted to link it to legends about Saint Boniface or Martin Luther, but these stories have no basis in history either. Our best historians think the Christmas tree tradition developed in the medieval period. During that time most people couldn't read or write, so plays were put on to teach biblical stories. One feature of such plays was a paradise tree representing the tree of knowledge (Genesis 2:9). In the play, the tree symbolized both the fallenness of humankind and the cross, the "tree" that brought us salvation. They decorated the paradise tree with apples for the fall and round pastry wafers for the Eucharist—the body of Christ that saves us. Interestingly, the Feast of Adam and Eve fell on December 24, so the public display of the paradise tree coincided with the day before the start of Christmas.

We don't know for certain how the medieval paradise tree became the Christmas tree we know today, but the paradise tree seems to have led to the cultural association between the decorated tree and the Christmas season. The first record of trees used in church and home decoration comes from sixteenth-century Germany. The Strasbourg cathedral displayed a fir tree (*Tannenbaum*) in 1539, and by 1611 Strasbourg locals were putting up fir trees in their homes, decorating them with paper roses, dried apples, wafers, and candies. By the 1640s the practice was so popular that one German theologian complained about it in writing. "Whence comes the custom, I know not," he says. "It is child's play. . . . Far better were it to point the children to the spiritual cedar-tree, Jesus Christ."[1] (Notice that even in the seventeenth century some Christians were worried about holiday trappings outshining Christ at the center of Christmas.)

Beginning with upper class urbanites, the Christmas tree trend spread throughout the population so that it was considered essential to German Christmas by the start of the nineteenth century. Aristocrats outside of Germany began displaying their own decorated Christmas trees, most notably Queen Victoria in 1848, and the trend quickly took hold among Protestants in Scandinavia, England, and North America. The tradition's popularity was helped along by marketing in newspapers and magazines, as well as its inclusion in Christmas-themed short stories. By the turn of the twentieth century, the Christmas tree was considered an essential tradition for most in the Western world.

For hundreds of years, Christian households made decorations—most of which were edible—for their Christmas trees by hand. If you've ever strung popcorn and cranberry garlands, you've joined in this long-standing tradition. The first commercial Christmas ornaments were produced in Germany in the 1860s. Woolworth's five-and-dime stores started selling their glass ornaments in the 1880s and the trend exploded in the United States. Lighted outdoor displays, first a feature of business buildings, became a feature of private home decorating in the 1950s and '60s.[2] Touring local Christmas light displays developed into a beloved family tradition for many households. By the twenty-first century, consumers could add inflatable yard decorations (Santa Clauses, snowmen, and even scarf-wearing dragons), color-changing LED lights (some timed with accompanying music), and many other options.

We might love our Christmas trees and accompanying decorations (I know I do!) but given this history it's also wise for Christians to be wary of thoughtless participation in such consumption. Maybe we could find better uses for our surplus funds—particularly during a season when we're called on to remember the poor. We need wisdom and discernment for such decisions.

But as with the Christmas gift-giving ritual, I'd like to suggest that maybe there's more going on here. Maybe my little sister was on to something, along with everyone who delights in Christmas decorations. Let's consider the words of the collect for the second Sunday of Christmas:

> O God, who wonderfully created, and yet more wonderfully restored, the dignity of human nature: Grant that we may share the divine life of him who humbled himself to share our humanity, your Son Jesus Christ; who lives and reigns with you, in the unity of the Holy Spirit, one God, for ever and ever. Amen.[3]

First, notice the reference to sharing the divine life, which recalls the great exchange theme discussed in chapter two. But also notice that God "wonderfully created, and yet more wonderfully restored, the dignity of human nature." The theme of creation and re-creation is central to both the biblical story and the Christian theological tradition. Not only did God create the cosmos, God is also re-creating it through Christ by the Spirit. When God joined himself to creation through Christ, all of creation was altered at its roots—redeemed, restored, and elevated to a status even beyond its former glory.

So what are we doing exactly when we decorate for Christmas? What are we doing when we cover our homes, yards, and businesses with tinsel, holly boughs, and twinkling lights? We are beautifying these places. We are adorning them with celebratory splendor—we might even say we are rendering them sacred. To decorate something is to affirm it as worthy of special acknowledgment. To decorate something is to call it good. And to name the world "good" is a reminder of both the truth of creation—"God saw that it was good" (Genesis 1:10)—and the truth of new creation: "I am making everything new!" (Revelation 21:5). Maybe it was this promise of future glory to which my sister, Leah, was so attached.

God's own creation can be seen as the work of adornment. Genesis says God filled the expanse above with stars and planets and brought forth crawling, chirping, swooping lifeforms to fill the earth. As God did so, gilding the dark with his artistry, God called his creation good.[4] Later God's people would ornament space in God's honor too. Solomon's temple, where the people of Israel met with God, was beautifully decorated, adorned with carvings of cherubim, palm trees, and open flowers overlaid with gold (1 Kings 6:29). The decoration of the temple was a form of veneration, a declaration of its enduring value and the goodness of its purpose: a suitable meeting place for humankind and God. This practice continued in Jewish synagogues and the spaces where Christians met for worship. From very early on Christians instinctively adorned their worship spaces with beautiful images and symbols, which sought to usher gathered worshipers into God's presence.

Yet, someone might object, our world remains fallen. Sin has wreaked havoc on creation and darkened every human heart. Even now creation groans, Saint Paul says, longing to be redeemed (Romans 8:19-22). There is no denying this truth. Sin is real and its consequences are real. But the fallenness of the world and the sinfulness of humans within it do not nullify the overall goodness of what God made. The fact that God in Christ has seen fit to redeem the world testifies to its inestimable value in

God's eyes. We are wonderfully made and wonderfully restored. Thanks be to God!

Julian of Norwich was a fourteenth-century mystic-theologian who maybe understood the belovedness of creation and new creation better than anyone. In the fifth chapter of her book *Revelations of Divine Love*, she describes a moving vision about the created world:

In this vision he also showed me a little thing, the size of a hazel-nut in the palm of my hand, and it was as round as a ball. I looked at it with my mind's eye and thought, "What can this be?" And the answer came to me, "It is all that is made." I wondered how it could last, for it was so small I thought it might suddenly have disappeared. And the answer in my mind was, "It lasts and will last forever because God loves it; and everything exists in the same way by the love of God." In this little thing I saw three properties: the first is that God made it, the second is that God loves it, the third is that God cares for it.[5]

God made it. God loves it. God cares for it. This summarizes well the nature of God's goodness, and the goodness of what God has made. The early church fathers taught that it was always God's intention to dwell with his creation through the incarnation. That is to say, the Word made flesh was always the goal of God's creation. Sin complicated this mission but it did not take away God's eternal intention to be joined to the world and humankind forever in Christ.

Yes, sin is real and the world is fallen. But God still loves the world and us, and in Christ God is making all things new.

Living rooms and shop windows aren't the only places where decorations are meaningful features of Christmas. When Iraqi forces expelled the Islamic State from the predominantly Christian city of Mosul in 2017, the reinstitution of Christmas celebrations was a major symbol of victory. Worship was held at Saint Paul's Cathedral, the only functioning church in Mosul, for the first time in years. But the Christmas Eve gathering was bittersweet. The Islamic State had done extensive damage to Mosul and other Christian communities during their occupation. They looted, demolished, and burned both homes and churches, stealing anything of value and smashing Christian relics. The physical destruction, though, was surpassed by the destruction of the community. Faced with the order to convert to Islam, pay heavy taxes, or die, tens of thousands of Christians fled, leaving behind an even smaller minority community than was present before.[6]

But in 2017, Mosul's Christians celebrated Christmas Eve Mass once again. And decor played a major part. Outside the building a portrait of a Christian executed by the Islamic State was displayed in defiant honor. White- and gold-robed clergy and well-dressed worshipers chanted and prayed surrounded by white sheets covering bombed-out windows and vandalized walls. Candles, wreaths, and Christmas trees adorned the battered sanctuary, and a simple stone cross hung above the altar. Beyond the church walls, Christians had erected Christmas trees and nativity scenes amid the surrounding rubble. Given all they had faced (and continue to face), these hopeful decorations testified to the courageous and enduring faith of Christians in Mosul.

Most of us are far from experiencing the kind of persecution the Iraqi Christian community has endured. And our Christmas decor does not possess the poignancy or gravitas that was displayed in and around Saint Paul's Cathedral. But I think our impulse to decorate our spheres for the Christmas season—whether in Chicago, Illinois, or Mosul, Iraq—are, however imperfectly, imitating our Creator and blessing the created world we know is good. Perhaps our temporary and inadequate adornments are a small, halting gesture toward the cosmos-wide renewal we know God's Spirit is bringing about in Christ.

✦ ✦ ✦

However your household or church chooses to participate in the tradition of Christmas decorations, God's mission to redeem his good creation—and all people within it— remains central to the annual celebration of Christmas. The Scriptures appointed for the Christmas season help bring this theme home. In the previous chapter we discussed the much-loved nativity of Luke with its characteristic angels, shepherds, and songs. Less well-known, and certainly less appreciated, is the account of Jesus' circumcision and naming, mentioned only briefly in Luke's Gospel: "On the eighth day, when it was time to circumcise the child, he was named Jesus, the name the angel had given him before he was conceived" (Luke 2:21).

Though it had been observed for many years prior, the circumcision of Christ was officially given its own day of commemoration—January 1—at the Council of Tours in 567 CE. January 1 comes eight days after the birth of Christ, the day when the law of Moses required every male child to be circumcised (Leviticus 12:3). So it was also referred to simply as the octave (or eighth) day of Christmas. Some think it was first intended as a day of fasting to counteract pagan festivities around the beginning of the new year. During the medieval period, though, it became a feast day with its own mass. In more recent years churches have tended to downplay the circumcision aspect (one can imagine why) and focus instead on the naming of Jesus, which took place at the same time. So the 1979 Book of Common Prayer specifies January 1 as the Feast of the Holy Name of Our Lord, while the 2019 Book of Common Prayer commemorates both the circumcision and the holy name.

Whether they emphasized Jesus' circumcision, his naming, or both, church teachers often used the occasion to accentuate the fact that Jesus was a real human being of real flesh and blood. He was a true Israelite, a descendant of Abraham and David, who was taught the law and submitted to its observance from his earliest days. Through his obedience to the law, Jesus was undoing the disobedience of Israel and humankind in general, demonstrating his faithfulness to God where we have been unfaithful and fulfilling the law where we have left it unfulfilled.

Moreover, in the first shedding of Jesus' blood at circumcision, we see a foreshadowing of the full shedding of his blood on the cross. "You are to give him the name Jesus," the angel tells Joseph, "because he will save his people from their sins" (Matthew 1:21). Jesus is the Greek form of the Hebrew name Joshua (or Yehoshua/Yeshua), meaning "rescuer" or "deliverer." Thus, Jesus' circumcision prefigures his crucifixion, and we see in it a glimpse of his name's salvific meaning. The deliverer's blood is shed at eight days old, initiating him into the people of Israel so that he might later shed his blood on the cross, atoning for the sins of Israel and the whole world.

Considering all of the above, the 2019 Book of Common Prayer leads us to pray this way:

Almighty God, your blessed Son fulfilled the covenant of circumcision for our sake, and was given the Name that is above every name: Give us grace faithfully to bear his Name, and to worship him with pure hearts according to the New Covenant; who lives and reigns with you, in the unity of the Holy Spirit, one God, now and forever. Amen.

It is through Jesus' faithfulness, beginning with his circumcision, that we are empowered to "bear his Name" and "worship him with pure hearts." And it is because he was the true Israelite, faithful to the covenant God of Israel, that he was able to become the universal Savior for all creation and all humankind. The good world God made, sullied through the fall, has been reconciled and redeemed through the blood of Christ's cross.

There's an already-not-yet element to this reality, as our Iraqi sisters and brothers well know. In Christ God has saved us from sin, evil, and death. God's promised kingdom is truly inaugurated in Christ's life, death, and resurrection. New creation has begun within the shell of the old. But the culmination of creation's renewal remains in the future.

The already-not-yet of new creation is embodied in the Watch Night services of Black churches in the United States, observed on December 31, the seventh day of Christmas. Also called Freedom's Eve, the first Watch Night service was held in 1862, the night before President Abraham Lincoln's Emancipation Proclamation

was set to take effect on January 1, 1863. In ardent anticipation, Black women and men, enslaved and free, came
together in churches, in homes, and around secret
"praying trees" to watch and wait, worship and pray, for
the turning of the year.

At the time, enslaved African Americans rarely found
relief from the constant surveillance of enslavers, who
worried that religion would foment slave resistance. Slave-
holders wrote laws to restrict worship gatherings, but enslaved people gathered anyway. They convened secretly in
the woods, practicing their faith surrounded by brush and
trees, which became known as "hush arbors" (or "hush
harbors"). There, away from the vigilant eyes of enslavers,
they whispered, moaned, spoke, and, when they could
hold it in no longer, shouted for the Lord.[7]

Like their hush arbor meetings, the first Watch Night
service began around sundown and continued past midnight. But this time, two hundred and forty-three years
after the first enslaved Africans arrived on the shores of
North America, slavery was officially over. In the words of
Frederick Douglass, "It is a day for poetry and song, a new
song. These cloudless skies, this balmy air, this brilliant
sunshine . . . are in harmony with the glorious morning of

liberty about to dawn up on us." When the New Year finally dawned, the moment Douglass called the "trump of jubilee," gathered worshipers erupted: "Joy and gladness exhausted all forms of expression," he wrote, "from shouts of praise to sobs and tears."[8] Just as with the Hebrews under Pharaoh, the Lord had seen his people's misery, heard their cries, and came down to deliver them. African Americans were eager to preserve their hard-fought freedom by serving as soldiers in the Union Army. By the end of the Civil War, around 186,000 Black men had enlisted, including Douglass's own sons, Charles and Lewis.

As we now know, word of the Emancipation Proclamation's effects didn't reach all enslaved Black persons until June 19, 1865, in Galveston, Texas (now celebrated annually as Juneteenth). Moreover, the emancipation celebrated then was tenuous and limited, as slavery gave way to white supremacist terrorism through lynching and Jim and Jane Crow laws that enforced racial apartheid in the South. Indeed, the fight for African American freedom continues long after the first Watch Night service concluded—up to the present day. Today Black churches still gather for worship and prayer on Freedom's Eve, recalling the faithfulness of God in their journey toward liberation. After hours of singing and testimonies, congregants will bow in prayer minutes before the midnight hour, saying, "Watchman, watchman, please tell me the hour of the night." In return the minister replies, "It is three minutes to midnight," "It is one minute before the new year," and "It is now midnight, freedom has come."[9] As Chicago's Trinity United Church of Christ sings during their services,

> Look where God has brought us,
> look how far we've come,
> we're not what we ought to be,
> we're not what we used to be.
> Thank you, Lord, thank you, Lord,
> for what you've done!

Black Christians know well the tension of living in the already-not-yet. They know both the goodness of existence and the sin that mars and destroys. They have proclaimed and embodied the mystery of faith for generations: Christ has died. Christ is risen. Christ will come again. And it is when Christ comes again that we'll see sin fully judged, the nations fully reconciled, the world fully set right, and all things brought to their intended glory in

Christ. Until then, our words and deeds are small procla-
mations of God's future kingdom. Thus, the church prays
during Christmastide for the grace to faithfully bear his
name because we know we still await the fullness of the
new creation.

What does all this have to do with Christmas decorations? Beneath the tinsel and multicolored lights lies the
deeper truth to which it testifies: creation is good, human
life is good, and God is redeeming both in Christ. As
fallen as the world remains, acknowledging the goodness
of renewed creation through holiday decoration can be a
lifegiving practice. The Scriptures of Christmas tell us that
instead of saving his people *from* the world, God chooses
to save his people *and* the world. And God chooses to do
so in and through the world—the good world God
creates, loves, and cares for.

It is good and right to reverence the world and celebrate
it, especially during the Festival of the Incarnation. May all
such decorations—both the tasteful and the garish—
point us toward the God of creation and re-creation.

FOR FURTHER READING

Brunner, Bernd. *Inventing the Christmas Tree*. New Haven, CT: Yale University Press, 2012.

Julian of Norwich. *Revelations of Divine Love*. Translated by Elizabeth Spearing. London, UK: Penguin Books, 1998.

Holmes, Barbara A. *Joy Unspeakable: Contemplative Practices of the Black Church*. Second Edition. Minneapolis: Fortress Press, 2017.

5

God of Life and Light

From the time I was five years old through my high school graduation, I spent every December rehearsing and performing in the *Nutcracker* ballet. I performed a variety of roles over the years, including a precocious party girl, a toy soldier, a dancing snowflake, and a waltzing flower. The one role I did not enjoy was that of a rat. Apart from all the negative things we associate with rats (rightly or wrongly), the rats are decidedly the bad guys in the *Nutcracker* story. To make matters worse, the costume was essentially a lumpy bag of faux fur. It felt like dancing in a wool sweater. Performing that role, especially as an adolescent girl, was a true exercise in humility!

Based on the story by E. T. A. Hoffman and set to the music of Tchaikovsky, the *Nutcracker* story goes like this: during the family's Christmas party, little Clara Stahlbaum receives the gift of a nutcracker from her mysterious

Uncle Drosselmeyer. After the party is over, Clara sneaks out of bed and falls asleep cradling her nutcracker beneath the Christmas tree. As she sleeps, everything in the room becomes large (or she becomes small, depending on the version). She awakens suddenly having been set upon by the wicked Rat King and his rat minions. Roused by Clara's shrieks, the Nutcracker Prince comes to life and does battle with the rats, assisted by a troop of rifle-bearing toy soldiers in crimson uniforms. Together they slay the Rat King and defeat his army. In celebration, the Nutcracker Prince whisks Clara away to the Land of Sweets where the Sugar Plum Fairy and other beautiful figures regale them with their dancing and treats. At the end Clara awakens, realizing it was all a dream.

I loved dancing in the *Nutcracker* year after year. Tchaikovsky's music remains for me the soundtrack of the month of December. But there was something about the story that never quite sat right with me. The conflict with evil ends in act one, and the combat concludes in a haphazard, quasicomedic way. At one point in the battle Clara throws her shoe at the Rat King, temporarily distracting him, and the Nutcracker runs him through. The remaining rats flee in fear, a few dragging the still-twitching body of the Rat King along with them. Even as a child I felt this denouement came too early and too easily. I had seen real-life villains wreak havoc on the world, and I knew it would take more than a smartly thrown shoe to take them down. And yet this is one reason the *Nutcracker* ballet is so beloved. The story allows us to escape for a few hours into a dream world of simple solutions and happy endings. But deep down we know the defeat of evil is not that easy.[1] Would that it were.

✦ ✦ ✦

In 2012, ten days before the start of Christmas, just when ballerinas the world over were rehearsing for their performances, twenty-year-old Adam Lanza shot and killed twenty-six people at Sandy Hook Elementary School in Newtown, Connecticut. The slain were twenty children aged six and seven, and six adult staff members. Before arriving at the school, Lanza had also shot and killed his mother in her home. He ended his murderous spree by shooting himself in the head as first responders began to arrive.

I remember gathering in church the following Sunday, still in shock, struggling to listen to the Scriptures and pray the prayers. The sanctuary had already been adorned with Christmas greenery and gleaming lights. The chorus of the opening hymn declared, "Rejoice! Rejoice! Immanuel shall come to you, O Israel."[2] It was all too incongruous. Holding my two children, then two and three years old, I wept quietly, thinking of the parents who would be burying their children for Christmas. The senselessness and injustice were overwhelming. And ringing in my ears were the words of the prophet Jeremiah quoted in Matthew's Gospel:

> A voice is heard in Ramah,
>   weeping and great mourning,
> Rachel weeping for her children
>   and refusing to be comforted,
>   because they are no more. (Matthew 2:18)

As much as we enjoy escapist entertainment like the *Nutcracker*, we know evil is real, powerful, and impossible to defeat with manmade weapons. As much as we like to tell ourselves the right security system or the right gun will keep the darkness at bay, we know that to be human is to be vulnerable to harm. None of us will make it through life unscathed by the destructive forces of our fallen cosmos. Evil, like sin, is always crouching at the door (Genesis 4:7).

Any consideration of Christmas must face head-on the grim reality of our world. Yes, creation is good and existence is good. But such goodness exists side by side with chaos and desolation. Kindergartners are gunned down in their classrooms. Toddlers starve to death. Refugee women are raped. Boys are forced to become soldiers. Addicted men take their own lives in despair. What does Christmas have to say about such darkness and death?

On this matter, the liturgical calendar demonstrates a deep wisdom. After the celebration of Christmas Day, the church observes three successive days of commemoration: the stoning of Saint Stephen (December 26), the exile of Saint John the Apostle (December 27), and the slaughter of the holy innocents by Herod (December 28). The medieval church christened these three figures the *Comites Christi*, the Companions of Christ, whose respective stories embody three kinds of martyrdom. Saint Stephen, whom we've already discussed, voluntarily gave himself up to martyrdom and was executed by stoning. Saint John, according to tradition, was arrested, tortured, and exiled by pagans but not executed. His willingness to die, though, remains an example to all. The holy innocents, the children of Bethlehem, were those Herod executed in his effort to kill the promised king: they unknowingly died for Christ.[3]

Though it may strike some as odd that the church would commemorate these heartbreaking stories so near to the joyful Feast of the Incarnation, those acquainted with sorrow understand. God is near to the brokenhearted and saves those who are crushed in spirit (Psalm 34:18). God knows the evil and suffering that plague our world and has dealt with it decisively in Jesus Christ. In a world of darkness and death, the God revealed in Christ brings light and life.

But let's not rush too far ahead. Christmastide intentionally includes stories of terror and flight, murder and mourning. So let's listen carefully to the tale Matthew's Gospel tells after the birth of the Christ child:

> When they had gone, an angel of the Lord appeared to Joseph in a dream. "Get up," he said, "take the child and his mother and escape to Egypt. Stay there until I tell you, for Herod is going to search for the child to kill him."

> So he got up, took the child and his mother during
> the night and left for Egypt, where he stayed until
> the death of Herod. (Matthew 2:13-15)

"They" refers to the Magi, or wise men, who had come from the East to worship the newborn king. In the West, the Magi don't make an appearance in the church calendar until the Feast of the Epiphany on January 6. Even so, the wise men have become a feature of nativity displays and Christmas plays, songs, poetry, and more for a very long time. In some parts of the church they even have names: Melchior, Caspar, and Balthazar.[4] The Greek word *magi*, often translated "wise men," could mean many things, including philosophers, astrologers, priests, magicians, or sorcerers. The Magi are often called kings, though, because the early church read their story in conjunction with Psalm 72 and Isaiah 60, both of which speak of Gentile kings bringing tribute to Israel's king. Thus, early Christians began to conflate the Magi and kings to the point where we have a song declaring, "We, three kings, of Orient are."

Whatever their official roles, the Magi were caretakers of philosophical and religious knowledge that had developed in the region of Persia.[5] Based on their studies, they journeyed hundreds of miles to offer worship to the Christ child. I'll leave further discussion of the Magi for the season of Epiphany, but it's worth noting the Magi's auspicious visit: Gentiles from a foreign land, offering a potent sign of the coming of God's worldwide, multi-ethnic kingdom.

Along the way the Magi stopped in Jerusalem first, alerting Herod and his household to the Christ child's presence (Matthew 2:1-2). Then, with guidance from Israel's chief priests and scribes, they made their way to Bethlehem to offer gifts to Jesus (Matthew 2:5-8). After their departure, Joseph, like his counterpart in Genesis, has another divinely inspired dream. And when God speaks to him in dreams, Joseph listens. The first time he was told to take Mary as his wife because she was pregnant by the Holy Spirit, and he obeyed. The second time he's told to take his young family and flee the region. And he obeys again. Though little is known about Joseph beyond this chapter, it is clear he is a man attuned to God's voice and practiced at submitting to it—an ideal example for the child Jesus to follow.

The contrast with Herod couldn't be stronger. A tyrannical despot, Herod had already had his wife and three of his sons executed because he was convinced they were a threat to his reign.[6] The Magi's inquiry must have hit him like a thunderbolt: "Where is the one who has been born king of the Jews?" (Matthew 2:2). A child who is from birth the king of the Jews—the people over whom Herod was appointed ruler by Rome? It's no surprise he immediately concocted a plan to kill the boy. But when the Magi don't cooperate, sneaking back to the East after their visit, Herod takes matters into his own hands. Matthew says,

> When Herod realized that he had been outwitted by the Magi, he was furious, and he gave orders to kill all the boys in Bethlehem and its vicinity who were two years old and under, in accordance with the time he had learned from the Magi. (Matthew 2:16)

Though we don't have record of this event from non-biblical sources, the massacre is fully consistent with Herod's character and reputation. And careful readers of Scripture can't help but see behind Herod the shadow of Egypt's Pharaoh, who sought to eliminate the Hebrews (and Moses with them) by killing their baby boys. Herod, like Pharaoh and all tyrants before and after him, is an authoritarian seeking to preserve power. Thus, the haunting words of the sixteenth-century "Coventry Carol" ring out:

> Herod the king, in his raging,
> Chargèd he hath this day
> His men of might in his own sight
> All young children to slay.

God's provision of a dream narrowly saves Jesus' life as the holy family flees into the night. We can imagine the scene. The frenzy of gathering essentials, haphazardly stuffing things into bags and packs, followed by a hurried departure into the dark, ominous night. The crying child, the exhausted and terrified mother, and Joseph's heart leaping into his throat every time they pass a soldier. In this way the holy family—just a few days or even hours after celebrating with the Magi—flee their homeland and begin the eighty-mile walk to the border of Egypt.

Their fortunes take an abrupt turn between the Magi's wondrous visit and Herod's murderous plot. One minute they're surrounded by visitors from faraway lands, basking in the hope and glory of what God is doing in their midst. The next minute they are hunted and afraid, stealing away under the cover of darkness, refugees on the lonely road to Egypt. Almost as soon as the Word of God appears in the flesh, the darkness rises up and tries to extinguish it.

So they hide in Egypt and begin a new life in a strange land. We don't know for sure where the holy family lived during their time in exile. They may have settled in Alexandria, which had the largest Jewish settlement at the time. But the important thing is they managed to escape Herod's murderous reach.

We rejoice in God's provision and protection through the terror of their escape. But what about the families who were not warned? It's almost too horrifying to imagine. At the time Bethlehem was a small village with maybe a thousand inhabitants. Herod's massacre is estimated to have included about ten to thirty children. There are few things as terrible as the powerlessness of being unable to protect those you love. Millions of the disinherited throughout history know the feeling well. As peasant Jews in Roman-occupied territory, Bethlehem's families had little recourse against the force of Roman steel. They could only watch and wail in desolation, fulfilling, as Matthew notes, the words of the prophet Jeremiah:

> Rachel weeping for her children
> and refusing to be comforted,
> because they are no more. (Matthew 2:18)

Although Matthew says this event fulfills the words of the prophet, he does not ascribe divine origin to the Bethlehem massacre. Whereas in earlier verses he clearly says events happened to fulfill what Scripture had said (Matthew 2:15), in the slaughter of the innocents those words are noticeably absent. The death of Bethlehem's boys is Herod's doing, not God's.

Also, Matthew is not saying that Jeremiah predicted the massacre hundreds of years in advance. The prophecy he quotes comes from Jeremiah 31, which speaks of the return of the people of Israel from exile in Babylon. After a time of judgment, God declares his devotion to his people: "I have loved you with an everlasting love" (Jeremiah 31:3). God is going to gather the people of Israel and bring them back to their land. After referencing the weeping of Rachel, Jeremiah offers a promise:

> This is what the LORD says:
>
> "Restrain your voice from weeping
> and your eyes from tears,

for your work will be rewarded,"
 declares the LORD.
 "They will return from the land of the enemy."
  (Jeremiah 31:16)

But Matthew omits the divine promise when he quotes Jeremiah 31. Why is that? While the mothers of Jeremiah's day could anticipate a return from exile, the mothers of Bethlehem had no such remedy on the way. Their pleas to God remained unanswered in Matthew's Gospel, eventually joining the cry of Christ himself from the cross: "My God, my God, why have you forsaken me?" (Matthew 27:46). As a small child, God's Messiah fled Judea with his family. But it is only so that the next time around he can face death squarely and triumph over it. When the Christ child grows up, he will gather the girls and boys of Israel in his arms and proclaim God's blessing over them. As the holy innocents died involuntarily in the place of the infant Jesus, so the end of Matthew's Gospel reveals the innocent one dying voluntarily in the place of all. It is only in his victorious resurrection from the dead three days later that Rachel, and all weeping mothers, find hope. Death—even this kind of unthinkable death—does not get the last word.

So the Book of Common Prayer leads us to pray with the appointed collect for the holy innocents:

> We remember today, O God, the slaughter of the holy innocents of Bethlehem by King Herod. Receive, we pray, into the arms of your mercy all innocent victims; and by your great might frustrate the designs of evil tyrants and establish your rule of justice, love, and peace; through Jesus Christ our Lord, who lives and reigns with you, in the unity of the Holy Spirit, one God, for ever and ever. *Amen.*[7]

Notice we pray that God would receive all innocent victims and, simultaneously, that God would stop murderous despots and establish his kingdom marked by "justice, love, and peace." We're praying, *Please, Lord, embrace all innocent victims with your loving mercy. And at the same time put an end to the people and institutions who bring about their deaths, replacing them with your kingdom of justice, love, and peace.* This only happens finally and completely "through Jesus Christ," the one who has overcome evil, sin, and death. But, as too many understand, it is hard to hold on to this promise when praying over a child-sized coffin.

After the Sandy Hook massacre, mourners gathered in public places all over the world. They came together to lament and comfort each other. The city of Newtown had multiple such gatherings or vigils, including one attended by President Barack Obama. Whether explicitly religious or not, most of these gatherings were marked by several elements: silence, prayer, candles, and singing. The candles and singing stand out most prominently because of their overlap with the Christmas season. Christmas Eve services are often marked by handheld candlelight, which is shared person to person. The Christmas season is also marked by music and singing, traditionally called caroling. As small as these gestures might seem, in times of darkness, the people of God light candles and sing. These are acts of liturgical resistance in the face of evil's deadly assaults.

Of course, Christians first began lighting candles and lamps because they were the only light sources for homes and worship spaces. Their purpose was more practical at first, but over time, they took on symbolic significance. As a result, with the advent of electricity and the light bulb, most Christians continued to light candles as part of worship. In liturgical churches, you'll usually find at least two candles on the altar, one each for the divine and human natures of Christ. Sometimes a separate alcove in the sanctuary will contain rows of votive candles in front of a kneeler for personal prayer. During Advent, four candles are lit in succession, three purple (or blue) and one rose, one for each Sunday in Advent. Then, on Christmas Eve or Christmas Day, a large white candle called the Christ candle is lit as a sign of Christ's arrival. For households observing Christmastide at home, the Christ candle is lit every night throughout the twelve days until Epiphany (though some churches use the Christ candle during Epiphany too). Nonliturgical churches use candles in a variety of ways as well. Christians do this in part because it's tradition, and human beings enjoy keeping traditions. But also, the presence of lighted candles, whether on the altar or in our hands, reminds us vividly that Christ is the light of the world (John 8:12)— much more so than electric lights. When we light candles and watch the light illuminate the darkness, we are seeing with our eyes and saying with our bodies, *The Father is with us, Christ is among us, and the Spirit is here.*[8]

Historically, singing has functioned in a similar way. From the earliest days of the church, Christians chose to sing in the face of their suffering. The book of Acts relates how Paul and Silas were severely beaten and imprisoned in stocks for their work among the people of Philippi. Yet, "About midnight Paul and Silas were praying and singing hymns to God, and the other prisoners were listening to them" (Acts 16:25). The practice of singing continued through the ages anywhere faithful Christians suffered trials or persecution. It is mentioned in the stories of Perpetua and Felicity, the French Huguenots, the Ugandan martyrs, Saint Mark Ji Tianxiang, and Pakistani Christians today.

Devout Christian and civil rights activist Fannie Lou Hamer was especially known for her passionate and defiant singing. When she and her companions were arrested in Winona, Mississippi, in 1963, she was severely beaten by Sheriff Earl Wayne Patridge and his deputies. The beating was so bad that she lost vision in one eye and suffered permanent kidney damage. After being dragged back to her cell, her friend and fellow activist Euvester Simpson tended her wounds. Simpson related the hellish night to an interviewer this way:

> I sat up all night with her applying cold towels and things to her face and hands trying to get her fever

down and to help some of the pain go away. And the only thing that got us through that was that . . . we sang. We sang all night. I mean songs got us through so many things, and without that music I think many of us would have just lost our minds or lost our way completely.[9]

Singing was the lifeblood of the civil rights movement. Hymns, spirituals, and protest songs rang out in buses and marches, on sidewalks and courthouse steps, and in jail cells all over the nation. In the face of unrelenting evil, activists sang to keep darkness and despair at bay. Their singing was both a proclamation to others and an exhortation to themselves that wickedness would not win. And so it remains for Christians in many other treacherous contexts today. As we sing, we lift up our eyes to the hills, from whence comes our help: "[Our] help comes from the LORD, the Maker of heaven and earth" (Psalm 121:2).

The singing described above is usually spontaneous, even if the songs are spurred on by trying circumstances. But Christian devotion to singing during Christmastide took on a formalized structure in the Anglican tradition of Nine Lessons and Carols, a special service alternating between Scripture readings and Christmas hymns. The first such service was held in Truro Cathedral in Cornwall, England in the late nineteenth century, but it is popularly attributed to King's College, Cambridge. Wherever it started, the Nine Lessons and Carols service is now used by churches of various Christian traditions all over the world. Today, King's College, Cambridge, broadcasts its Lessons and Carols service every year on Christmas Eve, a tradition that began with the BBC in 1928.[10]

In addition to the Nine Lessons and Carols, contemporary churches have begun to offer Longest Night or Blue Christmas services. Technically these services take place during Advent, usually on the winter solstice, the longest night of the year (on or around December 21). But I think it's appropriate to mention them here as they are attempts to hold space for mourning amid the busy preparations for Christmas. Rather than upbeat songs of comfort and joy, Longest Night services present an intentional time for worshipers to grieve and lament, with spoken words and songs, the suffering they've endured. As many know from experience, the gaiety of the holiday season can be distressing and alienating for those mourning losses, whether of loved ones, jobs, homes, or dreams. Blue Christmas services are a modern innovation that seeks to come alongside those who suffer and help them keep faith in the dark.

Though Matthew doesn't give us the details, we know the holy family had to keep faith as they waited on God's direction in Egypt. Eventually, after Herod died, Joseph had another dream (Matthew 2:19). The angel told him again to get up and go—this time back to Israel. Just as before, Joseph obeyed immediately. They traveled back to their homeland, ready to resume life in Bethlehem. Yet Joseph got word that Herod's son Archelaus was now ruling in Judea, and he was afraid to go there. Joseph's instincts were correct. Another dream (and our historical records) confirmed that Archelaus inherited his father's murderous temperament. (In fact, he was so violent and oppressive that Rome eventually deposed and replaced him with someone else. If you're too violent and oppressive for the Romans, that's really saying something.) So rather than take up residence near another bloodthirsty king, Joseph retreats with his family to the rural, backwater town of Nazareth.

While it is comforting to imagine the holy family dwelling safely and quietly in the hills of Galilee, it's hard to forget the other sons of Bethlehem who were lost to Herod's sword. Why were the other parents not given a similar version of Joseph's dream? The child Jesus lives and grows up with his family; the others die a horrible death. Matthew doesn't speak to this conundrum or attempt to relieve the tension. Just as there is no way to make peace with the slaughter of the innocents, there's also no way to make peace with the Sandy Hook massacre. The truth is, theodicies—philosophical attempts to justify the ways of God to humankind—fall flat in the face of wailing parents and traumatized communities. Amid the worst our fallen world has to offer, we don't need clever logic or pious platitudes. We need the promises of God. They tell us it will not be this way forever. One day God will make all things new:

> Look! God's dwelling place is now among the people, and he will dwell with them. They will be his people, and God himself will be with them and be their God. "He will wipe every tear from their eyes. There will be no more death" or mourning or crying or pain, for the old order of things has passed away. (Revelation 21:3-4)

When he comments on the holy family's escape to Egypt, Matthew quotes the prophet Hosea: "And so was fulfilled what the Lord had said through the prophet:

'Out of Egypt I called my son'" (Matthew 2:15). Hosea 11:1 refers backward to Israel's miraculous exodus under the leadership of Moses. The exodus is a mighty revelation of God's loving preservation of God's son Israel from the violence of Pharaoh. When God rescues the people of Israel from Egyptian slavery, he is powerfully demonstrating his special love and covenant loyalty to them. By using Hosea's words to apply to Jesus, Matthew is showing his readers that Jesus fulfills Israel's story.

As the incarnate Son of God, Jesus is Israel in person. Because of his divine sonship, Jesus is protected and preserved by the same covenant loyalty of God. Just as God saved Israel from the wrath of Pharaoh, so also God saves Jesus from the wrath of Herod. And through his life, death, and resurrection, Jesus will enact a new exodus for all of God's people: an eternal kingdom of justice, love, and peace. This is the good news of the gospel amid times of suffering: The one who fled violence and lived as an exile in Egypt is also coming again to judge the world. He will overcome and set right not just the evils of Herod and Adam Lanza, but also the evil that runs through us all. Thus we pray with one of the collects appointed for Christmas Day:

O God, you make us glad by the yearly festival of the birth of your only Son Jesus Christ: Grant that we, who joyfully receive him as our Redeemer, may with sure confidence behold him when he comes to be our Judge; who lives and reigns with you and the Holy Spirit, one God, now and forever. Amen.[11]

While we await the day when our righteous judge returns to set all things right, the people of God light candles and sing, holding space for grief and lament even while looking forward with hope. Into a world of darkness and death, God in Christ brings light and life—even if we can't see it yet.

FOR FURTHER READING

Pope Benedict XVI. *Jesus of Nazareth: The Infancy Narratives.* New York: Image, 2012.

Saint Bernard of Clairvaux. *Sermons of St. Bernard on Advent and Christmas.* Anthem Publishing, 1909.

Lawson-Jones, Mark. *Why Was the Partridge in the Pear Tree? The History of Christmas Carols.* Gloucestershire, UK: History Press, 2011.

Conclusion

GOD OF THE CRÈCHE AND THE CROSS

Modern-day Bethlehem is situated in one of the most volatile regions of the world. Though Bethlehem is in Palestinian-controlled territory, in 2002 Israeli Defense Forces (IDF) occupied it as a part of Operation Defensive Shield. In response, Palestinian militants and citizens took refuge in the Church of the Nativity. The siege lasted over a month before it was finally brought to an end.

Afterward, a fifty-mile dividing wall was constructed around three sides of the city, cutting it off from the surrounding territories. Though it had been common for Christian worshipers to traverse the six miles between Bethlehem and Jerusalem during annual Christmas celebrations, that is no longer possible. Today, the place of

Christ's birth is separated from the place of his death and resurrection by multiple fortified checkpoints and concrete roadblocks.[1]

The literal geography of the life of Christ is now disjointed and disconnected, but we must not allow our liturgy or theology to end up the same way. The season of Christmas ought to be observed within the larger church calendar, which details the rest of Christ's life, death, resurrection, and ascension, as well as the story of Christ's body, the church. The full calendar helps us remember that the baby in the manger did not come simply to be cradled and adored. He came to live, die, and rise again for the redemption of the world. He came to inaugurate a new kingdom and to empower us to live within it. The Festival of the Incarnation is followed by Epiphany, Lent, and Easter—and by Pentecost and Ordinary Time too.

Placing Christmas in this larger context helps us resist the cultural tendency to freeze the cherubic baby Jesus in time, romanticized and sentimentalized beyond recognition. The God of the crèche is also the God of the cross. The God of the holy innocents is also the God of the empty tomb. And the God of the flight to Egypt now reigns as Lord of all. Only this expansive, all-encompassing story is truly good news for all humankind.

Of course, the same good news that brings hope to the world also threatens the powers and principalities of the present evil age. This is most apparent in countries where the practice of Christianity is constrained by the government. In China, for example, which has a long history of Christian persecution, churches have been under immense pressure since the government instituted its "Sinicization" of religion campaign in 2018. The five-year plan intentionally seeks to turn Christianity (and other religions) into an indoctrination tool for the Chinese Communist Party through "patriotic education" in churches, socialist values in sermons, and even revisions to the Bible. Despite these efforts, many churches have resisted and been officially closed, driven underground to worship in homes and small groups.[2]

For Chinese Christians, Christmas is a time of even more government repression. Plenty of Chinese citizens observe Christmas as a purely secular celebration, but both Protestants and Catholics approach the holiday expectantly as a time of mass awakening and conversion. Whether among state-controlled churches or house churches, Christmas worship involves the communal confession that Jesus Christ is Lord.[3] And as Roman authorities understood in the first century, if Jesus Christ is Lord, then the government is not. The Christmastide crackdowns in China suggest the communist government knows that the Christ child constitutes a profound threat to their power. Bonhoeffer, writing under the brutal tyranny of the Third Reich, says it well:

> The authority of this poor child will grow (Isa. 9:7). It will encompass all the earth, and knowingly or unknowingly, all human generations until the end of the ages will have to serve it. It will be an authority over the hearts of people, but thrones and great kingdoms will also grow strong or fall apart with this power. The mysterious, invisible authority of the divine child over human hearts is more solidly grounded than the visible and resplendent power of earthly rulers. Ultimately all authority on earth must serve only the authority of Jesus Christ over humankind.[4]

It's easy to see how Christ's authority undermines the absolute claims of oppressive regimes. It's less easy to see how the Christ child confronts and subverts other challenges to his authority. Left to our own devices, human beings have a tendency to fashion ourselves rulers of our own little kingdoms. Turned inward, concerned only with our own interests and those who serve them, we become oblivious to the pride, envy, and greed destroying us from within. At the social and political level, we have a tendency to fashion antagonistic in groups and out groups, with accompanying "us versus them" discourse, to secure identity and shore up power and wealth. From such poisoned soil grows racism and tribalisms of all sorts, which perpetrate untold damage on people and communities. Into all of this comes the Christ child, the humble Word made flesh, confronting our inhumanity and demanding our allegiance.

✦ ✦ ✦

In the Orthodox icon of the nativity, Mary and the infant Jesus are depicted in the center, reclining at the mouth of a cave in the midst of a rocky, inhospitable world. Christ is wrapped in burial clothes, foreshadowing his coming death. On the left side, the three Magi travel to see the child, following the star. Above, in heaven, angelic hosts hover, telling the good news to shepherds on the right side. Some versions of this icon include a shepherd who sits playing a flute, adding his humble tune to the chorus of angels above. Joseph sits in the bottom left, pondering what all of this means, while a diabolic figure seeks to fill his mind with doubts. On the bottom right, midwives are pouring water to cleanse the Christ child, born truly God and truly human. At the very top of the icon, a bright blue shape, sometimes called a mandorla, signifies the presence and glory of God. Emanating from the mandorla is a blue and white beam pointing all the way to the center where the Christ child lies, indicating his descent from heaven to earth.

In some versions of the nativity icon, it looks as though the heavenly beam is piercing the image, literally bisecting the icon and splitting open the world. This seems to me an apt picture for the coming of Christ. Yes, he brings tidings of comfort and joy. And thank God he does! But he also brings a piercing luminosity that exposes our sin and drives out the darkness. Like a skilled surgeon, God in Christ cuts away our cancerous parts and, by his Spirit, applies healing balm to make us both holy

Figure 1. Nativity icon

and whole. It's a prospect both glorious and terrifying—as the work of God always is.

> Almighty God, you have poured upon us the new light of your incarnate Word: Grant that this light, enkindled in our hearts, may shine forth in our lives; through Jesus Christ our Lord, who lives and reigns with you, in the unity of the Holy Spirit, one God, now and forever. Amen.[5]

Acknowledgments

I would like to thank my mom, Wendy Hunter, for teaching me how to celebrate Christmas long before I had any theological understanding of the season.

I would also like to thank Aubrey Buster and Christin Fort, dear friends who heard my first musings on this book and urged me to write it my own way.

Thanks also go to my friend Esau McCaulley for conceiving of the series and inviting me to contribute, as well as Ethan McCarthy and the whole IVP team for their work to make this project a success.

Finally, thank you to Ronnie for his faithful support, and our children, William, Emmelia, and Althea, for their patience and enthusiasm. May the light of God's incarnate Word be enkindled in our hearts and shine forth in our lives.

The Scriptures and Collects of Christmastide

What follows are the appointed Scriptures and collects of the Christmas season. I have followed the 1979 Revised Common Lectionary and, unless otherwise noted, the 1979 Book of Common Prayer.

CHRISTMAS DAY I

Psalm 96

Isaiah 9:2-4, 6-7

Titus 2:11-14

Luke 2:1-14 (15-20)

CHRISTMAS DAY II

Psalm 97

Isaiah 62:6-7, 10-12

Titus 3:4-7

Luke 2:1-14 (15-20)

CHRISTMAS DAY III

Psalm 98

Isaiah 52:7-10

Hebrews 1:1-12

John 1:1-14

SAINT STEPHEN—DECEMBER 26

Morning Prayer

Psalm 28; 30

2 Chronicles 24:17-22

Acts 6:1-7

Evening Prayer

Psalm 118

Wisdom 4:7-15

Acts 7:59–8:8

SAINT JOHN—DECEMBER 27

Morning Prayer

Psalm 97; 98

Proverbs 8:22-30

John 13:20-35

Evening Prayer

Psalm 145

Isaiah 44:1-8

1 John 5:1-12

HOLY INNOCENTS—DECEMBER 28

Morning Prayer

Psalm 2; 26

Isaiah 49:13-23

Matthew 18:1-14

Evening Prayer

Psalm 19; 126

Isaiah 54:1-13

Mark 10:13-16

FIRST SUNDAY AFTER CHRISTMAS

Psalm 147

Isaiah 61:10–62:3

Galatians 3:23-25; 4:4-7

John 1:1-18

THE CIRCUMCISION AND HOLY NAME OF OUR LORD JESUS CHRIST—JANUARY 1

Psalm 8

Exodus 34:1-8

Romans 1:1-7 or Philippians 2:9-13

Luke 2:15-21

Second Sunday After Christmas

Psalm 84

Jeremiah 31:7-14

Ephesians 1:3-6, 15-19

Matthew 2:13-15, 19-23 or Luke 2:41-52 or Matthew
2:1-12

Christmas Eve—December 24

O God, you have caused this holy night to shine
with the brightness of the true Light: Grant that we,
who have known the mystery of that Light on earth,
may also enjoy him perfectly in heaven; where with
you and the Holy Spirit he lives and reigns, one God,
in glory everlasting. Amen.[1]

The Nativity of Our Lord:
Christmas Day—December 25

O God, you make us glad by the yearly festival of the
birth of your only Son Jesus Christ: Grant that we,

who joyfully receive him as our Redeemer, may with sure confidence behold him when he comes to be our Judge; who lives and reigns with you and the Holy Spirit, one God, now and forever. Amen.

or

O God, you have caused this holy night to shine with the brightness of the true Light: Grant that we, who have known the mystery of that Light on earth, may also enjoy him perfectly in heaven; where with you and the Holy Spirit he lives and reigns, one God, in glory everlasting. Amen.

or

Almighty God, you have given your only-begotten Son to take our nature upon him, and to be born [this day] of a pure virgin: Grant that we, who have been born again and made your children by adoption and grace, may daily be renewed by your Holy Spirit; through our Lord Jesus Christ, to whom with you and the same Spirit be honor and glory, now and forever. Amen.

Saint Stephen—December 26

We give you thanks, O Lord of glory, for the example of the first martyr Stephen, who looked up to heaven and prayed for his persecutors to your Son Jesus Christ, who stands at your right hand; where he lives and reigns with you and the Holy Spirit, one God, in glory everlasting. Amen.

Saint John—December 27

Shed upon your Church, O Lord, the brightness of your light, that we, being illumined by the teaching of your apostle and evangelist John, may so walk in the light of your truth, that at length we may attain to the fullness of eternal life; through Jesus Christ our Lord, who lives and reigns with you and the Holy Spirit, one God, for ever and ever. Amen.

The Holy Innocents—December 28

We remember today, O God, the slaughter of the holy innocents of Bethlehem by King Herod. Receive, we pray, into the arms of your mercy all innocent victims; and by your great might frustrate the designs of evil tyrants and establish your rule of justice, love, and peace; through Jesus Christ our Lord, who lives and reigns with you, in the unity of the Holy Spirit, one God, for ever and ever. Amen.

FIRST SUNDAY AFTER CHRISTMAS DAY

Almighty God, you have poured upon us the new light of your incarnate Word: Grant that this light, enkindled in our hearts, may shine forth in our lives; through Jesus Christ our Lord, who lives and reigns with you, in the unity of the Holy Spirit, one God, now and forever. Amen.

THE CIRCUMCISION AND HOLY NAME OF OUR LORD JESUS CHRIST—JANUARY 1

Almighty God, your blessed Son fulfilled the covenant of circumcision for our sake, and was given the Name that is above every name: Give us grace faithfully to bear his Name, and to worship him with pure hearts according to the New Covenant; who lives and reigns with you, in the unity of the Holy Spirit, one God, now and forever. Amen.[2]

or

Eternal Father, you gave to your incarnate Son the holy name of Jesus to be the sign of our salvation: Plant in every heart, we pray, the love of him who is the Savior of the world, our Lord Jesus Christ; who lives and reigns with you and the Holy Spirit, one God, in glory everlasting. Amen.

SECOND SUNDAY AFTER CHRISTMAS DAY

O God, who wonderfully created, and yet more wonderfully restored, the dignity of human nature: Grant that we may share the divine life of him who humbled himself to share our humanity, your Son Jesus Christ; who lives and reigns with you, in the unity of the Holy Spirit, one God, forever and ever. Amen.

Notes

AN INTRODUCTION

[1] Annie Dillard, *For the Time Being* (New York: Alfred A. Knopf, 1999), 79. The fourteen points on the star signify the three sets of fourteen generations in the genealogy of Jesus Christ according to Matthew's Gospel.

[2] Elizabeth Monier, "Bethlehem and the Middle East," in *The Oxford Handbook of Christmas*, ed. Timothy Larsen (Oxford, UK: Oxford University Press, 2020), 424.

[3] Madeleine L'Engle, "First Coming," in *The Ordering of Love: The New and Collected Poems of Madeleine L'Engle* (New York: Convergent, 2005).

[4] An allusion, of course, to Dr. Seuss's *How the Grinch Stole Christmas* (New York: Random House, 1985).

1. THE ORIGINS OF CHRISTMAS

[1] Clement of Alexandria, *Stromateis* 1.21.145.

[2] Rosh Hashanah 11a, The William Davidson Talmud, Sefaria, www .sefaria.org/Rosh_Hashanah.11a?lang=bi, accessed December 4, 2022.

[3] Augustine, *On the Trinity* 4.5.9, www.newadvent.org/fathers/130104 .htm, accessed December 4, 2022.

[4] Paul F. Bradshaw, "The Dating of Christmas: The Early Church," in *The Oxford Handbook of Christmas*, ed. Timothy Larsen (Oxford, UK:

Oxford University Press, 2020), 3-13. See also Andrew McGowan, "How December 25 Became Christmas," *Bible Review* 18, no. 6 (December 2002): 46-48.

[5] Mary Ellen Hynes, *Companion to the Calendar: A Guide to the Saints and Mysteries of the Christian Calendar* (Chicago: Liturgy Training Publications, 1993), 8.

[6] For more information see Stephen Nissenbaum, *The Battle for Christmas: A Social and Cultural History of Our Most Cherished Holiday* (New York: Vintage Books, 1997).

[7] Nissenbaum, *The Battle for Christmas*, 7.

[8] For more on this story, see Andrew R. Holmes, "Reformed and Dissenting Protestants," in *The Oxford Handbook of Christmas*, 167-79.

2. GOD OF THE GREAT EXCHANGE

[1] Ellen M. Litwicki, "Gifts and Charity," in *The Oxford Handbook of Christmas,* ed. Timothy Larsen (Oxford, UK: Oxford University Press, 2020), 277-85.

[2] G. Dautovic, "Christmas Spending Statistics: Deck the Halls with Boughs of Money," Fortunly, updated December 23, 2021, https://fortunly.com/statistics/christmas-spending-statistics/#gref.

[3] C. B. Wheeler, "Gifts," *Living Age* 242 (September 24): 794-99, quoted by Litwicki, "Gifts and Charity," 283.

[4] *O admirabile commercium*, ChoralWiki, Choral Public Domain Library, https://cpdl.org/wiki/index.php/O_admirabile_commercium, accessed September 26, 2020.

[5] St. Athanasius of Alexandria, *On the Incarnation,* trans. John Behr, Popular Patristics Series (Yonkers, NY: St. Vladimir's Seminary Press, 2012), 19.

[6] For a summary of the various backgrounds suggested by scholars for understanding "the Word" in John's Gospel, see Leon Morris, *The Gospel According to John*, rev. ed., New International Commentary on the New Testament (Grand Rapids, MI: Eerdmans, 1995), 63-70.

7 St. Augustine of Hippo, Sermon 191, *Sermons*, vol. 6, trans. Edmund Hill, ed. John E. Rotelle (New Rochelle, NY: New City Press, 1993), 42-45.

8 St. John Chrysostom, "The Joys of Christmas," in *The Living Testament: The Essential Writings of Christianity Since the Bible* (New York: Harper & Row, 1985), 72.

9 Order of Mass, no. 37, The Roman Missal (United States Conference of Catholic Bishops, 2011), 542.

10 Pope Benedict XVI, "Nativity of the Lord: Mystery of Joy and Light," General Audience Address, Vatican, January 4, 2012, www.vatican.va /content/benedict-xvi/en/audiences/2012/documents/hf_ben-xvi _aud_20120104.pdf.

11 Joel Cabrita, "Africa," in *The Oxford Handbook of Christmas*, 507.

12 Chris Marchand, *Celebrating the Twelve Days of Christmas: A Guide for Churches and Families* (Eugene, OR: Wipf & Stock, 2019), 74-75.

13 Book of Common Prayer, 1979, 213.

3. God of the Poor

1 For a brief discussion of the debate surrounding the origins of this famous and much-beloved Filipino Christmas song, see Nicai de Guzman, "Was 'Ang Pasko Ay Sumapit' Stolen from Two Cebuano Musicians?" *Esquire*, January 3, 2018, www.esquiremag.ph/culture /music/was-pasko-na-naman-stolen-from-two-cebuano-musicians -a1729-20180103-lfrm.

2 Gustavo Gutiérrez, *The God of Life*, trans. Matthew O'Connell (Maryknoll, NY: Orbis Books, 1991), 85.

3 Chris Marchand, *Celebrating the Twelve Days of Christmas: A Guide for Churches and Families* (Eugene, OR: Wipf & Stock, 2019), 91.

4 Martin Luther, *Martin Luther's Christmas Book*, ed. Roland H. Bainton (Minneapolis: Fortress, 2017), 60.

5 Thomas Aquinas, *Summa Theologiae* II-II, q. 32., a. 2.

6 Luther, *Christmas Book*, 15.

[7] Jean-Marc Éla, *My Faith as an African,* trans. John Pairman Brown and Susan Perry (Maryknoll, NY: Orbis Books, 1988), 105.

[8] Luci Shaw, "Made Flesh," in *Accompanied by Angels: Poems of the Incarnation* (Grand Rapids, MI: Eerdmans, 2006), 26. Reprinted by permission of the publisher; all rights reserved.

[9] Pope Benedict XVI, *Jesus of Nazareth: The Infancy Narratives,* trans. Philip J. Whitmore (New York: Image, 2012), 72.

[10] St. Bernard of Clairvaux, *Sermons on Advent and Christmas* (London: Anthem, 2020), 128.

[11] Dietrich Bonhoeffer, *The Mystery of the Holy Night* (New York: Crossroad, 1997), 43.

4. GOD OF CREATION AND RE-CREATION

[1] David Bertaina, "Trees and Decorations," in *The Oxford Handbook of Christmas,* ed. Timothy Larsen (Oxford, UK: Oxford University Press, 2020), 267.

[2] Ace Collins, *Stories Behind the Great Traditions of Christmas* (Grand Rapids, MI: Zondervan, 2003), 73-77. See also Bertaina, "Trees and Decorations," 265-75.

[3] Book of Common Prayer, 1979, 214.

[4] Thanks to Jane Williams for this beautiful thought in *Approaching Christmas* (Oxford, UK: Lion Press, 2005), 39-42.

[5] Julian of Norwich, *Revelations of Divine Love,* trans. Elizabeth Spearing (London: Penguin Books, 1998), 47.

[6] The full story is that Christians began to flee the country when the US-led invasion of Iraq began in 2003. By 2014, estimates are that 90 percent of Mosul's Christian population had already fled, leaving behind only two thousand families when it was captured by the Islamic State. See Mohammed Salim, "Iraq's Mosul celebrates first post-IS Christmas," *AFP,* Yahoo News, December 24, 2017, www.yahoo.com/news/iraqs-mosul-celebrates-first-post-christmas-140959011.html.

[7] Barbara A. Holmes, *Joy Unspeakable: Contemplative Practices of the Black Church,* 2nd ed. (Minneapolis: Fortress Press, 2017), 45-66.

[8] "The Historical Legacy of Watch Night," National Museum of African American History and Culture, https://nmaahc.si.edu/blog-post /historical-legacy-watch-night, accessed January 7, 2023.

[9] "Historical Legacy of Watch Night," https://nmaahc.si.edu/blog -post/historical-legacy-watch-night.

5. GOD OF LIFE AND LIGHT

[1] Fleming Rutledge inspired me to think more deeply about the *Nutcracker* story in *Advent: The Once and Future Coming of Jesus Christ* (Grand Rapids, MI: Eerdmans, 2018).

[2] "O Come, O Come, Emmanuel," trans. J. M. Neale, 1851.

[3] Joseph F. Kelly, *The Origins of Christmas,* rev. ed. (Collegeville, MN: Liturgical Press, 2014), 93.

[4] This tradition has been traced to a Greek manuscript apparently composed in Alexandria in the sixth century, which was translated into Latin as *Excerpta Latina Barbari*. The text claims, "At that time in the reign of Augustus, on 1st January the Magi brought him gifts and worshipped him. The names of the Magi were Bithisarea, Melichior and Gathaspa." See "Excerpta Latina Barbari," Attalus, www.attalus.org /translate/barbari.html, accessed January 8, 2023.

[5] Pope Benedict XVI, *Jesus of Nazareth: The Infancy Narratives*, trans. Philip J. Whitmore (New York: Image, 2012), 92-94.

[6] Benedict XVI, *The Infancy Narratives*, 108.

[7] Book of Common Prayer, 1979, 238.

[8] Inspired by the liturgy of the Anglican Church of Kenya. For the text and contextual exposition, see Graham Kings and Geoff Morgan, eds., *Offerings from Kenya to Anglicanism: Liturgical Texts and Contexts Including 'A Kenyan Service of Holy Communion'* (Cambridge, UK: Grove Books, 2001).

[9] Euvester Simpson, "Euvester Simpson Oral History Interview Conducted by John Dittmer in Jackson, Mississippi, 2013 March 12," Civil Rights History Project Collection, Library of Congress, www.loc.gov/item/2015669171.

[10] "History of a Festival of Nine Lessons and Carols," King's College, Cambridge, copyright 2023, www.kings.cam.ac.uk/chapel/a-festival-of-nine-lessons-and-carols/history-of-a-festival-of-nine-lessons-and-carols.

[11] Book of Common Prayer, 1979, 212.

CONCLUSION: GOD OF THE CRÈCHE AND THE CROSS

[1] Elizabeth Monier, "Bethlehem and the Middle East," in *The Oxford Handbook of Christmas*, ed. Timothy Larsen (Oxford, UK: Oxford University Press, 2020), 430.

[2] Alice Su, "For China's Underground Church, This Was no Easy Christmas," *Los Angeles Times*, December 25, 2019, www.latimes.com/world-nation/story/2019-12-25/china-church-sinicization.

[3] Joseph Tse-Hei Lee, "Asia," in *The Oxford Handbook of Christmas*, 519.

[4] Dietrich Bonhoeffer, *God Is in the Manger: Reflections on Advent and Christmas,* trans. O. C. Dean Jr., ed. Jana Riess (Louisville, KY: Westminster John Knox, 2010), 68.

[5] Book of Common Prayer, 1979, 212.

APPENDIX: THE SCRIPTURES AND COLLECTS OF CHRISTMASTIDE

[1] Book of Common Prayer, 2019, 599.

[2] Book of Common Prayer, 2019, 600.

The Fullness of Time Series

E ach volume in the Fullness of Time series invites readers to engage with the riches of the church year, exploring the traditions, prayers, Scriptures, and rituals of the seasons of the church calendar.